FOUL DEEDS AND SUSPICIOUS DEATHS AROUND DERBY

Foul Deeds and Suspicious Deaths Around

DERBY

KEVIN TURTON

Series Editor
Brian Elliott

Wharncliffe Books

First Published in 2005 by
Wharncliffe Books
an imprint of
Pen and Sword Books Limited,
47 Church Street, Barnsley,
South Yorkshire. S70 2AS

Copyright © Kevin Turton, 2005

For up-to-date information on other titles produced under the
Wharncliffe imprint, please telephone or write to:

> **Wharncliffe Books**
> **FREEPOST**
> **47 Church Street**
> **Barnsley**
> **South Yorkshire S70 2BR**
> **Telephone (24 hours): 01226 734555**

ISBN: 1-903425-76-x

Printed and bound in England
By CPI UK.

Pen & Sword Books Ltd incorporates the Imprints of Pen & Sword Aviation, Pen & Sword Maritime, Pen & Sword Military, Wharncliffe Books, Pen & Sword Select, Pen & Sword Military Classics and Leo Cooper.

For a complete list of Pen & Sword titles please contact
PEN & SWORD BOOKS LIMITED
47 Church Street, Barnsley, South Yorkshire, S70 2AS, England
E-mail: enquiries@pen-and-sword.co.uk
Website: www.pen-and-sword.co.uk

Printed in the United Kingdom by
CPI UK

Contents

Introduction

When '*...each murder trial was conducted beneath the shadow of the executioner.*'

Death, in whatever guise, is devastating for those around it. Those people, be they family or friends, have to pick up the pieces of their own lives and move forward into the waiting years beyond. But if that death has been caused by an act of violence, then that loss is more pronounced. Those left behind must steal themselves to be shocked by the manner of the death and if that death is proved to have been either murder or simply declared suspicious, then they must also be prepared to have their own lives stripped bare.

Suspicion always falls on those closest to the victim. Police know that in most cases of this type the person killed has often known the killer. It is a fact that a great number of murder victims fall prey to someone they know, or have known extremely well, which makes the crime of murder not only odious but also strangely compelling. Family and friends, those very people mourning the loss, often find themselves under close scrutiny. It is the manner in which they have lived their own lives up to the point at which murder has taken place that often becomes public property. There is no escaping the public gaze if suspicion casts its shadow across the life of anyone associated with a violent crime involving death that eventually enters the courtroom. Dissemblance is not an option afforded to any that enter the gladiatorial arena where lives are broken open and those brought to account are faced with their accusers.

Today a whole network of reporters from the attractive face of television, the distance of radio and the daily familiarity of our morning newspaper, are bent on giving us as much detail as possible about all the lives probed by the bewigged offices of both defence and prosecution. We are abhorred by the crime they discuss, horrified by the violence they describe and at the same time wholly fascinated by the detail they manage to uncover. We are, to all intents and purposes, compelled to watch or listen and often do both. So, is today so very different from that period of our collective past that lies beyond the reach of modern memory? No, apart from the technology that has allowed a different and more varied type of media to grow around our own lives, we have retained the same fascination our grandparents once held. Some would say we are more obsessed than any previous generation. News has a voracious appetite and our preoccupation with it appears to grow. In turn, that means we are perhaps a little more ambivalent about this type of crime than ever we used to be. Nevertheless our interest has not waned over the years.

In *Foul Deeds and Suspicious Deaths Around Derby* all the cases investigated, covering a period between 1818 and 1944, also dominated the public's attention though mainly through the written word. A small army of reporters carefully recorded the events of both inquests and trials. At the former they were careful to lay before their readership as much anecdotal information as they could in order to set the scene for the developing police investigation. In the latter they were meticulous in the reporting of any proceeding murder trial. What each case has in common, however, that is not relevant to today, is the very crucial fact that each murder trial was conducted beneath the shadow of the executioner.

No matter what your viewpoint is on capital punishment in the period this book covers there was never any debate. Society at the time of every crime examined in the following pages was a very different society from that in which we all live today. Murderers paid the ultimate price for taking a life. No liberal view had extinguished the right of a court to send a convicted murderer to the gallows. Technology had also not advanced to the level where media news coverage had become a voracious monster, whose insatiable appetite needed to be fed on a diet of facts from around the world. Life, some would argue, was simpler then if not more brutal. Reports of murder were uncommon and therefore demanding of an audience, unlike today when the audience is perhaps less demanding of the reportage or its quality.

Judge as you will but there is no doubting the fact that all the people involved in the cases that make up this book once held a fascination for the people of Derby and its shire. The events in their lives that once brought notoriety and sorrow in equal measure to a public stage are stories that still tug at the public conscience. Part of the fabric of Derby's history and its social and historical past, these same events paint a vivid picture of a people living within a society we no longer understand. They tell a story just as they once did from the freshly printed page of the newspaper that fell onto the doormat each and every morning. The story is one of human emotion as moving today as it was all those years ago. Each of the following pages represents a glimpse into a fascinating if gruesome past. Enjoy the book but more importantly enjoy the journey on which it will take you.

And as you do so I must take a moment to thank those people who have contributed through their time and effort to help me bring this book to the bookshelf. Derby Local Studies Library in particular and all the staff that work within its walls have been extremely kind. No information was too difficult to obtain and their help was freely given. Thanks are due to Ruth Gordon, for pointing me in the right direction when I sought county images and also to Paul Hudson and Nick Tomlinson for setting up these images for my use. The *Derby Mercury* deserves credit for its numerous and enlightening reportage of the crimes I have investigated and Maureen Yule does for her unstinting support and photographic expertise. To others, too numerous to mention, I thank for help and expertise when it was needed, no matter how small my request.

Chapter 1

A Tragic Case of Poisoning – The Murder of Jane Grant
1818

It was a cold and a very calculated murder.

Sixteen-year-old Hannah Bocking had lived all her short life in the small village of Litton. Educated by the parish to a rudimentary level, the main substance of which had centred around the ability to read, she had attained perhaps more than most. Born into a poor family struggling to maintain any reasonable kind of living from Derbyshire's harsh moorland peaks, she had been put to work well away from home at an early age. The lack of parental guidance during her formative years, was what the *Derby Mercury* eventually blamed for her fall from grace. Had she been able to remain within the bosom of her family then, argued the newspaper, she would never have strayed far from the security of home and would almost certainly have never appeared in Derby court charged with murder.

Whether true or not is probably a debateable point but Hannah Bocking did stray, administering poison to her very good friend Jane Grant. It was a cold and very calculated murder. Hannah had purposely bought poison (exactly which type was never recorded), but

Derby Gaol c1810. www.picturethepast.org.uk

having made the purchase, she then kept it carefully hidden away for over ten weeks. This may have been because she was unsure of herself or perhaps believed that a change of circumstance would remove the need to use it. Jane, no doubt unaware of how her friend felt toward her, had once been Hannah's close friend. When she accepted a position in the village that Hannah believed had rightly belonged to herself, she unknowingly put her life at risk. It was that action that had prompted the purchase and quite probably the long wait before it had been put to use had been because Hannah earnestly believed her friend would see sense. When it became clear that Jane was not about to acquiesce to her friends jealousy the poison was taken back out of its secret hiding place. Carefully, she added it to a cake mixture. This seemingly innocuous cake she then offered up as a gift and Jane, believing her friend had at last reconciled herself to the situation, accepted it gratefully. What better way to commit murder than to do it in such a way as to remove all suspicion from herself. Leastways that was how Hannah saw it. She never believed anyone would realise that the cake had been poisoned and had been the cause of a good friend's death.

The unfortunate young woman died in absolute agony over a period of days and despite Hannah's belief to the contrary it was she that fell under immediate suspicion. Jane Grant had eaten nothing else before falling ill other than the gift she had received. Everyone pointed the

The stocks at Litton. The author

finger in Hannah's direction. When it became clear that she had purchased poison all those weeks earlier she was arrested and, after Jane's inevitable death was charged with murder.

During her long incarceration in Derby Gaol she made no act of contrition, showed little remorse and expressed no sorrow for the death of her friend. The appearance she made in court in March of the following year was reported as being without a flicker of emotion and on receiving the sentence of death she had looked around the courtroom impassively. According to Hannah Bocking it had not been she who bought or administered the poison. That distinction, she claimed, had been earned by her own sister and supported by most of her own family. No one of course believed it and she probably knew they never would.

A narrow street at Litton today. The author

After the trial, a number of, what the *Derby Mercury* described as benevolent ladies, visited her condemned cell. Concerned for her plight and her young age they desperately wanted her to recant these accusations and make peace with her own family.   In this they had some success. On the morning of her execution in conversation with the prison chaplain she finally accepted her own guilt. After seeking religious absolution and withdrawing all the accusations she had made against her family, she made a full and frank confession. The *Derby Mercury* made great use of it in its reportage of the final stages of her young life. After her execution before a huge Derby crowd her body, in accordance with custom, was delivered up for medical dissection.

The newspaper made one wry observation. Hannah Bocking had, they pointed out:

> *... Resided in a remote and retired part of Derbyshire, and nearly all those who have suffered for many years past on account of violent and outrageous offences have lived in similar situations.... The civilisation of the towns seems more favourable to the virtue of their inhabitants in*

Litton church. Author's collection

these points of view than even the villages of our county, however unfriendly they may be to morals in other respects. Will not the same observation be found true of all large associations of individuals, excepting perhaps the metropolis of the kingdom and a very few of our overgrown manufacturing towns?

Chapter 2

The Price of Fame – The Death of Highwayman Thomas Hopkinson
1819

There was to be no confessing of his sins.

Born in 1799 in Ashover, Thomas Hopkinson ought to have grown into a church-going, conscientious and hardworking member of the community. Unfortunately, for the people of Derby and the surrounding area, what he became was the absolute opposite. Born into a weaving family, he was taught to read and write, learn his catechism and to attend regular Sunday services at the parish church. By the age of fourteen he had developed a significant skill at the loom and, as far as his family were concerned, his future had been successfully plotted. Then along came Thomas Jackson. Two years older, the son of an uncaring father who had absconded from the family home whilst he was still very young, he was a little more worldly wise than his younger friend. Knowledge of Derbyshire's criminal fraternity had enabled him to earn a living far away from the restrictions of manual labour. Never seemingly wanting for money and with an apparently wide circle of friends about him, he had begun to

South West view of Derby County Gaol. www.picturethepast.org.uk

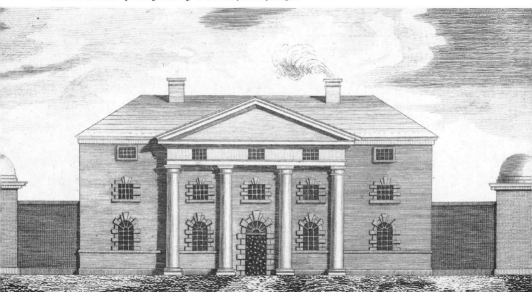

An Account of T. Hopkinson,

Who was lately EXECUTED at DERBY,

FOR HIGHWAY ROBBERY:

Enumerating a Catalogue of Offences he remembered to have committed up to that period.

ON Friday week, a young man, named T. HOPKINSON, underwent the awful sentence of death on the front of Derby Gaol, after a career of guilt, which, although short, seems to have been marked by an extraordinary degree of profligacy. He was but twenty: and from the age of fourteen, he confessed, to the best of his recollection, to have committed the following offences :—

Cutting at five different times horses manes and tails, and two cows' tails ; cutting off the feet of a living sheep in the turnpike-road ; two highway robberies ; breaking into butchers' shops three times, and stealing whole sides and joints of mutton ; breaking into one house, one shop, one pantry, two corn mills, and one turnpike-house, and stealing flour, meat, clothes, money, &c. : robbing gardens 27 times ; stealing one poney ; stealing poultry 95 times, 209 fowls, 21 geese, 9 ducks, and 14 turkies ; stealing at 32 times, 65 pecks of wheat ; stealing at 20 times, 92 rabbits ; stealing at 20 times, 11½ pecks of potatoes ; stealing at 20 times, 18 sheep and 3 lambs, and skinning one alive ; milking cows in the night time belonging to 66 persons ; stealing at 4 times, 105 pigeons out of dove-cootes ; setting fire to a corn-stack, and attempting to fir hers on several occasions.

was added an almost incalculable number nor offences ; so that scarce a day seemed to ve elapsed, from the commencement of his guilty career, without some offence having been committed, the fruits of which were spent in the worst debauchery.

was finally condemned at the last Assizes, for highway robbery, having previously turned King's evidence against four of his companions, for setting fire to the stacks of hay and corn in the farm-yard of Colonel Halton, all of whom were executed. This wretched youth was a weaver ; and, up to the age of fourteen, was brought up in great propriety. He then became acquainted with a youth named Jackson, one of those who terminated his existence for firing the stacks of Colonel Halton, and by him was led on to the irregularities which we have described. Jackson was the son of a depraved father, who stood by while his son was launched into eternity, and who became a candidate for the office of executioner to Hopkinson. Hopkinson did not seem to feel the awfulness of his situation, and died without exhibiting any symptoms of remorse.

DELAY NOT.

HASTEN, O sinner ! *to be wise,*
  And stay not for the morrow's sun ;
The longer Wisdom you despise,
  The harder is she to be won.

O hasten, *mercy to implore,*
  And stay not for the morrow's sun ;
Who knows ? thy season may be o'er
  Before this ev'ning's stage be run.

O hasten, sinner, *to return,*
  And stay not for the morrow's sun,
For fear thy lamp should fail to burn
  Before the needful work be done.

O hasten, sinner, *to be blest,*
  And stay not for the morrow's sun,
For fear the curse should thee arrest,
  Before the morrow be begun.

Spirit of God, the sinner turn,
  Now rouse him from his deathful state !
O may he not thy counsel spurn,
  Nor rue his fatal choice too late.

LONDON : Printed and sold by J. & C. Evans, Long-lane, West Smithfield.

Broadsheet of Thomas Hopkinson's execution. Derby Local Studies Library exert an influence upon the developing Thomas Hopkinson that would forever change his life.

By the age of fifteen young Hopkinson had become an accomplished poacher, spending long nights in fields across the county. He became extremely adept in the art of killing silently and discovered that he was able to sell all he killed. No time, then, for weaving and even less interest in the small amount of money it earned. Despite his father's protestations he began to spend more and more time away from home. The proceeds of his night poaching brought him greater opportunities; leastways that was how he viewed it. The money enabled him to break out of what he had come to view as drudgery and to travel freely around the county. It also meant he could indulge in as many licentious practices as his newfound wealth would allow. When he tired of these he simply moved on to other things and increased his criminal activity. By the end of 1814 he had begun to rob hen roosts and gardens to supplement his income from the illegal killing of game. Market forces dictated the most lucrative activities to be involved in. A network of buyers bought anything he stole and almost by design then ensured a greater need. In turn this led on to other crimes.

Petty pilfering and poaching eventually gave way to sheep stealing and with it a notoriety he could have managed without. His reputation went before him, which meant there were few places that welcomed his visits and ever more that wanted rid. Still in the company of Thomas Jackson, the two responsible by this time for a catalogue of crime stretching through almost every month of the year, it became inevitable that they would attract other like-minded criminals to their cause. King, Booth and Brown increased their number to five, which in turn increased their criminal activities but also lead to a greater internal strife. Little is known of these others but between them all they set out on a four-year reign of terror. Sheep stealing gave way to horse stealing and in turn to horse breaking, which led on to burglary and finally highway robbery.

Captured whilst alone in 1818, Hopkinson admitted horse stealing and was duly charged; the authorities not aware at that time of just whom they held in custody. But Hopkinson could not afford for them to discover his true identity. He knew that the longer he stayed where he was then the more likely someone would point a finger in his direction and he would hang. Distrustful of the man King, whom he believed would be on the end of that pointing finger, he decided to seize the moment first. Prior to his arrest all five of them had been responsible for destroying the crops of a Colonel Haton. They had set fire to all the haystacks and the gathered corn that lay in barns across

THE LIFE AND EXECUTION OF
THOMAS HOPKINSON, jun.

Who suffered this Day on the New Drop, in front of the County Gaol, Derby,

For Highway Robbery.

THIS unfortunate young man, only 20 years of age, was found guilty at the late Assizes in Derby, together with John Fletcher, of stopping William Bucknall upon the Turnpike Road near Dronfield, putting him in bodily fear, and taking from his person, a purse containing twelve shillings and six-pence.

The Criminal was born at Ashover, in this County, where he resided with his Father till he was fourteen years old. The family then removed to Woolley Moor, and here it was that he formed an intercourse with abandoned companions, and commenced that profligate career which brought him to his untimely end. In the number of his wicked associates were Thomas Jackson, jun. John King, John Brown, and George Booth, who were all executed two years ago for setting fire to stacks of hay and corn in the farm-yard of Colonel Halton. Thomas Hopkinson was an accomplice in this horrid crime, and was admitted King's evidence on the trial of his companions. Their dreadful fate afforded no salutary warning to Hopkinson, who proceeded in his guilty career till he committed the crime for which the judgment of the law has thus been awfully executed upon him.

His life, though a comparatively short one, has been marked by the commission of an incredible number of offences. Of these he made a confession during his confinement in the house of correction at Chesterfield, and they are more than sufficient to shew that his whole time was spent in the perpetration of almost every species of vice. The petty pilferings in which he first engaged, gradually led him on to bolder offences; his mind became so familiarised with guilt, that he seemed scarcely sensible of its depravity; and thus in the natural progress of iniquity, he was led on till he "was driven away in his wickedness."

On looking back to the history of his short but criminal course, his first transgressions may with great justice be referred to the wicked company of Thomas Jackson, who was his constant associate. After this intimacy had been formed, every moral feeling and every religious consideration were abandoned. He no longer read his bible, he no longer went to church; and thus the seeds of instruction which had been sown in his infant mind were choked and became unfruitful. Poaching, robbing hen roosts, gardens, and barns were the occupations of his nights; and his days were spent either in that kind of idleness which is ever the fruitful source of fresh crimes, or in dissipating in profligate excess the money acquired by his nefarious practices. Offences of a still heavier kind succeeded of course to those we have enumerated. Sheep stealing, horse stealing, house breaking, and highway robbery, marked the boldness with which he and his companions advanced in vice. They were indeed the terror and the reproach of their neighbourhood. After his condemnation, Hopkinson showed not much concern for his approaching fate. The sight of the unfortunate woman in the chapel, who was going to be executed on the 22nd of March, excited in him a stronger emotion than he expressed on any other account, but he was not capable of deep reflection, and seldom seemed sufficiently impressed with the awful situation in which he himself was placed.

It is no uncommon thing for persons, who come to an untimely and disgraceful end, to acknowledge upon the fatal scaffold, that a neglect of the Sabbath, laid the foundation of their ruin.

Between twelve and one o'clock this day, he was brought to the fatal spot, and having spent a short time in prayer, he was launched into eternity, amidst a vast concourse of spectators.

(G. WILKINS, PRINTER, QUEEN STREET, DERBY.)   *April 2d,* 1819.

Broadsheet detailing the life and execution of Thomas Hopkinson. Derby Local Studies Library his land and escaped without being seen. The crime had caused a huge uproar and he knew that to be convicted of it was a capital offence. Nevertheless, he made a deal with the court, a free pardon for all his crimes in exchange for the names of those responsible. The court readily accepted and he had no compunction in handing over his short list, including the name of Thomas Jackson, the friend who had taught him the life he had come to love. The four were quickly rounded up, tried and eventually executed.

At liberty once again, he perhaps ought to have reconsidered his life, made changes and gone off in a new and more acceptable direction. But Thomas Hopkinson was by this time a hardened criminal and what's more a criminal with a network of dealers to keep him in financial luxury. For him the decision to return to Highway robbery was a no contest and he did so wholeheartedly; it was to prove a serious miscalculation. Unfortunately arrest and imprisonment had brought with it an unwanted price, greater notoriety, and this time in the quarter that mattered most, the courts. He quickly became a wanted man and, as such, his name and face would inevitably condemn him, as it eventually did.

On 7 February 1819, in company with a fellow reprobate named John Fletcher, he attempted to carry out a highway robbery on the Derby road. It all went terribly wrong; he was identified and arrested within hours of the foiled attempt. Brought to trial at Derby in March, there was little he could offer by way of defence and at its conclusion he was sentenced to death by an uncaring court, which could hardly have come as a surprise to him. Languishing in Derby Gaol, he showed little by way of contrition, preferring instead to relate to any one who would listen stories of what he earnestly believed had been a series of adventures. Despite the joint pressures of church and prison, he refused to recant his past and insisted there had been nothing in his life that warranted execution. No crime, and he admitted there had been many, had been serious enough to force him onto the scaffold. There was to be no confessing of his sins.

On the morning of his execution, his father, whom he had not seen for some considerable time, visited him. The men talked together for an hour. It was a difficult meeting and the father, distraught at the thought of his son's impending death, left the cell in tears. But for Thomas the day appeared to hold no fear. After engaging in the religious observance usual on such occasions he expressed his forgiveness of every enemy he had and said his goodbyes to all those he had met in prison. Firm of foot, he then climbed the steps up to the scaffold, spoke with those he met along the way and then stood before the huge crowd which had gathered to witness his ignominious death. Addressing the cheering mob he twice proclaimed his innocence before the trap opened and he was lost to eternity.

According to the *Derby Mercury* whose reporter had detailed much of the events surrounding his death, a man who desperately wanted to put the rope around Hopkinson's neck had approached the authorities several days prior to the execution. That man was the father of Thomas Jackson, who had watched his son hanged almost a year earlier. Bitter and vengeful, he sought retribution for the fact that Hopkinson had betrayed his own son over the arson at Colonel Haton's farm. Claiming that in order to save his own life, Hopkinson had condemned his friend and as a consequence he, the father, ought to be allowed redress. He was, of course refused, but no doubt from his place amongst the Derby crowd earnestly believed justice had finally been done.

Chapter 3

Pity the Poor Children – The Murders of Elizabeth and Martha Smith

1835

'You should not have fetched me again after I ran away.'

Toward the end of April 1835, fourteen-year-old William Wild was sent to work for Joshua Smith at Church Broughton. A small farmer, he needed help around the house and someone fit enough to take charge of his small number of cattle. A married man, he and his wife Ann had three young children and his mother-in-law Elizabeth Hall living in, so the household was rarely quiet and a spare pair of hands was always needed. Unfortunately for the Smiths, William was far from enamoured of being sent from his home to live and work amongst strangers. Neither did he like the kind of work he was being asked to do, particularly by the women. Used by them as a general domestic servant with occasional nursery duties, he began to resent his role and saw household chores as an affront to his masculinity. After two weeks he

Church Broughton parish church. The author

ran away and returned home. But he was to find no solace before his parent's hearth. Angered at his sudden arrival on their doorstep and realising their sudden loss of income should they allow him to stay, they simply turned him around and sent him back. So by the middle of May, when William walked back into the Smith household, the family were receiving into their midst a bitter and much aggrieved young man.

Not that it appeared to have made a deal of difference. William's role in the house remained unchanged and, from his return, he was expected to pick up were he left off. Household tasks remained as they had been when he left and the resentment that had caused him to break out for freedom remained unchecked and unnoticed. Sadly for the Smiths they were to pay a price for this lack of observation. It was a price they most certainly did not deserve but one that was exacted nevertheless.

On 22 May at about three o'clock in the afternoon William, after having just fed the pigs and being set the task of cleaning the house fire irons, was ordered out to go and bring home the two youngest children. Ann Smith's mother, Elizabeth Hall, wanted them back in the house so that they could be fed and then settled down for the night. She had little regard for William or his feelings. To her he was a domestic servant, no more and no less, and as such he did as he was bid. William of course refused, telling her in no uncertain terms that it was not his role to go chasing after children. The two clashed but Elizabeth had the weight of the Smith family opinion behind her. Recognising the futility of his argument he gave in and in a petulant display of slighted youth threw the fire irons to the floor and stormed out of the house.

Elizabeth watched him walk across the village toward a fallen tree that lay behind Thomas Fearn's house. Just beyond could be seen the bobbing heads of a number of small children playing around the trunk. Amongst the group were the Smith's eldest son aged seven and their two little girls, Elizabeth aged three and Martha aged one. These two William was to bring back with him. But William was angry; incensed by what he saw as nursemaids' work he was not about to bring the girls straight back home. Telling the others in the group where they could find a number of birds' nests he sent them scuttering off along a hedgerow whilst he scooped Martha under an arm and grasped Elizabeth by the hand. Walking off in the opposite direction he took the two to Ox Close a short distance away and sat them beside what was known locally as The Pit. This was a pond that lay beneath a steep bank, normally out of bounds to the children. William knew it well.

The Holly Bush *(public house).* The author

Sitting his two charges on top of the bank no more than a foot or so from the edge he then went off in search of wild flowers. When he returned the two children had moved closer to the edge than was safe but he made no attempt to bring them to a safer place and instead pushed them into the water. Standing on the bank side he then watched them drown and when satisfied they were dead he returned to the Smith house.

Ann Smith was washing clothes in the yard when she saw him cross the stile at the bottom of the field and as he passed her he told her that he could not get the two children to come home. According to him, they cried so much he left them behind and she would have to fetch them later herself. Unperturbed by what he had said and not in the least suspicious that anything was wrong, she carried on with her washing. There was no great urgency as she saw it, despite her mother wanting the children back before evening, particularly with her husband Joshua in Derby farming market with no expectation that he would arrive home until the following day having the house settled before their evening meal mattered less than on other days. So she waited until she had completed her chores before setting out herself.

No children were around the Fearn's house or the fallen tree when she arrived at the place where she thought they had been left. Walking through a gap in the hedgerow she then went on to The Pit. There beneath her feet she could clearly see the body of Elizabeth floating face down in the water. She screamed for help and William was first on the scene. Within minutes had found the second dead child, Martha, where he had known she would be from the moment he began his search. By this time other children had gathered and Ann sent one of them off to find William Earp and his wife who lived the nearer to where she stood. William, meantime, she sent off to find local surgeon James Adams. But William of course had no intention of finding any kind of surgeon, local or otherwise, and after finding a secluded spot far enough away from prying eyes, he sat for three hours. When he did eventually return, it was to tell the assembled family and neighbours that the doctor would not come. They were to rub the children with salt in his absence. He was instantly accused of lying, someone in the crowd that had grown around the dead bodies shouted that he had never been for a doctor. Ann Smith, believing that he had murdered the two little girls, shouted out accusingly. 'How could you do such a thing?' William, in a slip of the tongue that was to cost him dear, turned on her angrily. 'You should not have fetched me again after I ran away.'

It was enough confirmation for most that the drowning may not have been accidental and that William must have had a hand in it. The spiteful reply he gave Ann Smith had already condemned him in the ears of all who heard it. But no evidence meant no arrest and William was allowed to remain free. That freedom, however, was to be short lived.

The inquest opened at the public house at Church Broughton the following morning. Landlord Mr Adams had allowed the bodies to be laid out in his back room and the hearing, though brief, drew few conclusions. What it did do, however, was point an accusing finger at the last person to have seen the girls alive. William Wild had tried to tell any that would listen that he had not deliberately killed them. The girls, he insisted, had tumbled into the water when his foot had slipped as he returned with flowers to the place where they had sat on the bank. Caught by his own left foot as he fell, he had unintentionally pushed the two into the water below and had had no means by which to pull them out. Local farmer, Mr Wragg, unimpressed by the story but aware of the build up of animosity against the young man, took it upon himself, after the inquest, to carry out an arrest. William, more for his own safety than for any other reason, was secured in the parlour of Mr Adams, public house. Here both men asked him if he had killed the girls. Understandably perhaps, William was less than willing to co-operate and refused to answer. It took several hours and the agreement of the farmer to leave the house before he was prepared to even discuss the previous day's events. But, once alone with the landlord, he finally confessed that the girls had not slipped at all but that he had placed them in the water knowing that they had no chance of escape. He had then watched as the two had drowned.

The trial opened in Derby on 30 July before Sir Stephen Gaselee and a packed courtroom, people having travelled from far afield to hear the grisly and appalling details of the double murder. William pleaded not guilty and offered in mitigation the fact that death had been the result of an accident. Unfortunately for him, after the court had heard exhaustive evidence as to his state of mind at the time caused by his forced removal from his maternal home, of the argument with Elizabeth Hall and from numerous neighbours who had clearly seen him with the two girls on his way toward The Pit, there was little he could do to counteract the growth of damning evidence against him but in his statement to the court he attempted to show that he was innocent:

> *I was…alone with two children near the pit; they were about three yards from the pit when I left them to get some ladysmocks (wild flowers); I was two or three minutes away doing this; when I returned back I found that they had got nearer to the pit; they had just sat down before I had got the last ladysmocks; they were sitting close together about three quarters of a yard off the edge; as I was returning. Martha being the nearest to me, and Bessy just going to kiss her or clip her, I stumbled against Martha and sent her into the pit first, and Bessy immediately after, my left foot did it all. Bessy had hold of Martha behind with her arm round her waist; I ran up from the side nearest the lane where I had been getting ladysmocks up to the side where the tree is, and they were sitting together between the lane and the tree; I went sharpish, as hard as I could walk, and with me catching my foot it hurled me on one side; it hurled me toward the edge. I meant to have come between them and the pit but I just caught my left foot; they were facing the pit; I caught them behind with my foot; they neither of them made any noise in the water but kept sailing on like a fish in the water. I tried to catch hold of their clothes with a hooked stick, which soon came off…*

It had a ring of truth about it but William had not gone in search of the doctor when, later, the bodies had been found and he had made no serious attempt to drag the girls out of the water. These two factors alone counted against him most seriously.

The jury took only a short time to return a guilty verdict. The judge, somewhat moved by the story of the deaths and by the young man's age spoke to William of his great sorrow at the position in which both of them had been placed and of his mental torment in being confronted by what he believed to be the truth of the case:

Vernon Gate, site of some of Derby's executions. The author

> *...I have looked with an earnest endeavour at the various deposi-tions, to ascertain whether or not something in the shape of palliation had arisen- whether I could see just reason to view the case as one of manslaughter, but there was no part of them which would in any way bear me out in putting such a construction on the proceedings...You were either guilty of wilful murder or totally innocent. The jury have however rightly decided. A more cruel and unprovoked murder never came before my observation...You made no attempt to rescue them, but regarded them while in the act of drowning.*

Placing the black cap upon his head, he then turned back to William Wild and pronounced sentence of death upon him.

Chapter 4

An Unnecessary Killing – The Murder of Martha Goddard

1835

The scene inside was one of utter destruction and carnage.

Twenty-four-years-old John Hulme had been a chimney sweep all his life, augmenting his income as a travelling tinker from time to time. But money had always been in short supply and the tinker business had only ever really been evidenced if he had carried out a local burglary. The idea of travelling was only a cover for him to escape prying eyes when necessary and perhaps even sell on stolen goods. By the early 1840s he had formed a thieves partnership with two colliers, Samuel Bonsall and William Bland, both hardened criminals with convictions for robbery and both local to where he lived in Heage. Only two years older than Hulme, Bonsall had already evolved into an accomplished thief but had a tendency to be more violent than his partners, so it was often left to Bland to dictate just when and where they carried out a robbery. At thirty-nine-years-old he was the elder statesman of the trio, not that age gave him any serious rights, just perhaps a louder voice than the others.

On 29 September 1842 William Bland arrived at Hulme's house with Bonsall in tow. The two had been discussing the possibility of carrying out a robbery at Stanley Hall, some six miles from Derby. Bland had decided that the idea had merit. He knew that the Hall was

The road into Heage today. The author

only occupied by two spinsters, known locally as the Misses Goddard, and that there were with no resident servants. Eccentric and single, Sarah and her sister Martha had lived in the Hall for over forty years. Well connected, born of a Tideswell clergyman, they held land and property and were connected with some of the richest families in England. The fact that they had always refused to employ servants unless absolutely necessary (in which case they used people from the nearby village of Stanley) and had divided the house up between them, was all part of their eccentricity. To those living locally who had grown used to seeing the old ladies carrying out their own chores, their quirkiness merely added to their charm. To Bland it also made them extremely vulnerable to robbery. Unknown to him until told over a few beers in a nearby pub, it had not taken long for him to realise the potential their strange existence offered him. Bonsall needed little convincing and after listening to Bland explain the vulnerability of the Hall neither did Hulme. Nevertheless, despite all this information, the three still armed themselves extremely well before setting out. As if expecting to be attacked by a regiment of foot soldiers, they took with them wooden staffs, whose rounded ends had been overlaid with lead, as well as a poker and a two-foot long crowbar.

Arriving at the Hall in the early hours of 30 September John Hulme clambered onto the roof of the coal house, more of a lean-to that attached itself to one side of the house than a constructed building.

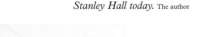

Stanley Hall today. The author

After removing a number of slates, he slipped quietly into the small bunker and pushed open the door into the main residence. The intention had been that he would unlock the main front door to allow the others in. Unfortunately for him Sarah Goddard, who unlike her sister had not retired to bed, had heard his efforts. As Hulme stumbled into the house he met the old lady clutching a candle. He struck out the moment he saw the light, catching her on the right side of her head. Screaming at him as the candle fell from her grasp he then struck a second time. Battered and bleeding badly Sarah made a dash for the stairs. Panicked by her sudden appearance and uncertain of where she was going in the darkness he gave chase, finally catching her on the landing where he struck her again several times before she lay quietly on the floor.

After returning downstairs to draw the bolts he told the other two that he had been forced to beat one of the sisters, but that she was alive and upstairs. Bonsall needed no further explanation. Telling Hulme the old lady would tell them where the money was, he went running up the stairs to find and confront her. He discovered her, still on the floor, blood streaming from a series of head wounds but having crawled into a bedroom. Standing over her with the crowbar in his hand he demanded she hand over all the households money. He wanted only five pound notes or gold and silver. Scared out of her wits she offered what she could, some fifteen shillings, and told him there was no more. Disbelieving and by now desperate he then drew a knife from his belt and threatened to cut her throat if she did not reveal the whereabouts of the house's wealth. Sarah, distraught and fearful of her life pleaded with him to go, offering him food or clothes but insisting there was no money.

At that point and whilst the other two where ransacking the other rooms of the Hall, Martha, into whose room Sarah had managed to crawl, called out to her sister and tried to raise herself from the bed. The sudden movement and disembodied voice startled Bonsall. In a fit of panic he turned away from the prostrate Sarah and ran toward the dark silhouette by now sitting up in bed. Without a moment's hesitation he struck out at it several times, striking the shadowy figure about the head, neck and body. Unable to defend herself, poor old Martha Goddard had no chance of avoiding the blows and despite her screams was quickly beaten to death.

The three then gathered in the doorway of the Hall; they had managed between them to collect two shawls, a quantity of linen, pieces of a lady's gown, a large piece of pink and black cloth and some thirty shillings in cash. These they quickly stuffed into a cloth bag,

The outbuildings used by the killers. The author

known as a rag gatherer, and ran off down the lane toward Heage. Unfortunately for them, within half an hour of leaving the Hall, and at a little after 2.30 am, they were met by local farmer, Joseph Roe. It was an accidental meeting but one with profound results. He recognised the three, not by name but certainly by sight and even challenged them about being out at so late an hour. As they parted Bonsall wanted to turn back and kill him. Only the intervention of William Bland saved the man's life.

Arriving back at Heage they all descended on Hulme's house where seventeen-year-old Richard Dronfield, the apprentice sweep that shared the rooms, was roused from his bed. He made breakfast and stoked up the fire as the little group of conspirators emptied out their ill-gotten gains across the floor. Removing their outer clothing they all

The lane where Hulme, Bland and Bonsall met farmer Joseph Roe after the murder.
The author

then set about removing the various bloodstains they had all acquired during the robbery. Once satisfied they were clean again, the money was divided up equally and the rest of the robbery proceeds were stuffed back into the bag to be buried in nextdoors garden until they felt it safe to retrieve them.

Back in Stanley, the alarm was raised after the badly bruised and battered Sarah Goddard had managed to make her way to her nearest neighbour. William Scattergood lived no more than one hundred yards away from the Goddards. When Sarah arrived at his door, she was in severe shock and still bleeding heavily but managed to rouse him from his bed. He in turn did what he could for her and then allowed her to take him back to the Hall. The scene inside was one of utter destruction and carnage. Blood stained the floors, stairs and walls and poor old Martha lay propped up by pillows, still in her own bed but obviously dead. A later examination took place by local surgeon, Robert Boden, who described her wounds as being centred about the top of her head, all of which had fractured her skull in several places and there was a severe cut above the left eye, causing much of the blood loss.

A reward of £200 was instantly offered and a promise of pardon tendered, except to the man who committed the murder. The three men of Heage were suddenly thrust to the forefront of every police enquiry in Derbyshire. Bonsall was the first to realise that they were all falling under suspicion and arrived at Hulme's house some five days later warning they all should leave and hide away somewhere safe. It was also decided that the bag containing the items they had stolen should be moved. Hulme, along with his young apprentice, agreed to dig it up and take it to Ambergate and there rebury it. Bland and Bonsall then went their separate ways.

All could have gone well had not Hulme, on the following day, in a conversation with his near neighbour, needle maker, Joseph Simpson, admitted his culpability and named his accomplices. Simpson had always known that Hulme had been a thief and having just returned from Derby that very morning where he had heard of the murder and robbery quite naturally raised the subject as the two men talked. Hulme, taken by surprise at how quickly word of the killing had spread probed his neighbour for greater detail and in the process gave himself away. Not satisfied with merely confirming his own involvement he then went on to tell Joseph Simpson just how the robbery had been committed and exactly who had been involved, naively trusting his neighbour to keep the conversation private and not report it to the relevant authorities. It was a mistake for which he was to pay heavily.

After reburying the bag, he went to his mother's house at Leek in Staffordshire where few knew him and stayed several days. Word then arrived from Derby that Bland had been caught in possession of a brown apron which had come from the Goddard house and which he ought not to have retained. He, in turn, had named Bonsall who was arrested the same day and both had named Hulme. With that knowledge in mind and realising he was about to be caught in the police net he ran away and hid in nearby woodland. There he stayed for two months evading capture and stealing food.

Whilst all that was going on his young apprentice, perhaps because of a growing awareness in his own involvement and wanting to avoid conviction as an accessory, dug up the stolen goods a third time. He took them to Derby police and he made the first statement that would implicate the three men in murder. This was eventually supplemented by statements made by two prisoners both of whom had shared a cell with Bland and Bonsall for a number of days after their arrest.

William Salt, a shoemaker of Ashbourne, told police in his statement that Samuel Bonsall had confessed to the robbery and the fact that Martha Goddard had been murdered, but he accused Bland of being the murderer. John Brown on the other hand, in prison for stealing a cow, gave a contradictory statement and insisted that it had been Bonsall who had wielded the crow bar. Bland, he told police, had related much of the detail of the crime including John Hulme's attack on Sarah Goddard during their brief stay together. But when the conversation had turned to murder he had been emphatic in his accusation against Bonsall.

Not that it mattered greatly to the police. They knew by the beginning of November that all three men had carried out the break-in and, therefore, by association if nothing else, were all guilty of murder. They were content to bring all to justice and allow a jury to decide just who had made the fatal blows. With that in mind they intensified their search for John Hulme and were rewarded when he was finally discovered in his woodland hideaway on 20 November. He was initially taken to Leek where he was imprisoned for a short period, arriving back in Derby in early 1843.

The trial opened on 20 March that same year and such was the interest throughout the shire that the courthouse was besieged from 7 am onwards. In fact, so desperate were people for admittance, they even stormed the court after the doors had been closed due to lack of capacity, forcing them open and causing the judge to forcibly eject them once again. Undeterred, they had then clambered onto the roof and thronged around every available window, which gave them a view of proceedings and allowed them to hear the odd word expressed by the various counsel. Apparently content, and not prepared to relinquish such hard won ground, there they stayed for the duration of the trial. The judge, Mr Baron Gurney, took his seat at nine o'clock and all three prisoners were brought to the dock. All pleaded not guilty.

From the outset it was plain that all had been involved in the robbery. The items recovered by the young chimney sweep, Richard Dronfield, were all produced in open court and throughout the morning identified as having belonged to Stanley Hall by a long line of witnesses. The sisters may not have employed live in servants but over the years they had employed the people of Stanley village in sufficient quantities for there to be enough who knew the women's personal belongings by sight. For over forty years some of the women of the village had been regular attendants at the Hall. There was little they did not know about the Goddards so proving robbery was never an issue, proving murder, however, was far more difficult. Though the court seemed to accept that because all three had been involved in the break-in then one of the group had certainly carried out the killing. It was never contended that they were innocent of the charge just that none of them would confess to murder. Individually, throughout their incarceration, each had accused the other, a very deliberate ploy, according to crown prosecutor Mr Sergeant-Clarke, but it did nothing, he insisted, that would save them from the gallows:

> …*With regard to the law of the case, if any number of persons went out to commit a felony, and to resist with violence, if violence was used and murder ensued, all were equally guilty. Now, before the prisoners went out, they made preparations; taking with them a razor knife, and staffs, which proved the design to resist with violence, if needed, while engaged in the robbery. The jury would recollect the resistance expected could only be from two aged ladies; and they would draw their own conclusion from the taking of the weapons alluded to.*

He was right. The only difficulty the jury were ever likely to have had was in trying to apportion blame for the killing. This, the crown prosecutor addressed in this speech and therefore gave them the opportunity of returning a guilty verdict against all without having to hold a deliberation amongst themselves. After seven hours of evidence, none of which was in mitigation, they took only fifteen minutes to reach their inevitable decision. All were pronounced guilty and sentenced to death.

Upwards of 40,000 people turned out in Derby on a cool April morning to witness a triple drop. So great were the numbers that they

Friar Gate today. The author

filled the whole of Vernon Street and spilled out into much of Friar
Gate. Roads, gardens, yards, housetops and any other vantage point
were overflowing with people desperate to see the executions first
hand. A Mr Bally, artist of Manchester, had been hired to record the
day's relevant images and Derby sculptor, Mr W Barton, was to take
plaster cast impressions of the prisoners' faces after execution. Derby's
theatre announced it would open after the hangings to entertain those
that had travelled in from the surrounding countryside, such was the
carnival atmosphere that surrounded the three men as they walked
onto the scaffold at midday to be met by their executioner, Heywood
of Appleby. None addressed the crowd and, as the traps opened, for
the only time that morning, a stillness swept across the faces of those
gathered across the wide concourse.

The only postscript to the murder came after the bodies had been
removed when it was revealed that Samuel Bonsall had admitted his
guilt just minutes prior to leaving the prison that morning. In a
confession to the prison chaplain he told him that it had been he that
struck down Martha Goddard.

Chapter 5

A Case of Insanity – The Murder of Ann Cross

1847

...he took a knife from the kitchen...and stabbed her to death.

Thomas Cross had probably always been a man with a psychotic temperament but when he and his wife Ann met and later married, she had probably ignored all the signs. In 1825, one year later, pregnant with her first child Matilda, she was made starkly aware of her husband's shortcomings when he stormed out into the night dressed only in his nightshirt. It took three neighbours to restrain him and forcibly carry him back to the house in Derby. At first diagnosing typhus, doctors embarked upon a course of treatment the result of which sent him spiralling out of control and into an ever-increasing mental decline. Realising their error, a decision was finally made, some months after the initial signs of madness had appeared, to send him to the Spring Vale Lunatic Asylum. Ann Cross was left in a severe predicament, heavily pregnant, short of money and with no-one close at hand to help nurse her through her first confinement she was forced to leave the family home and return to her parents. Daughter Matilda was eventually born safely and toward the end of that same year, after being told that Thomas had recovered sufficiently to be allowed back into society, she made the return to Derby.

The two lived peaceably

Victoria Street, Derby in 1840. Derby Mercury

St Peter's Street c1900. www.picturethepast.org.uk

enough for the next few years, a second daughter Louisa being born in 1830. But Thomas was never again the same man. A further period of irrational behaviour took place in 1838, which resulted in him being forced to leave his job and for the next few years life turned ever more difficult for the family. Once again Ann was forced to wait out his recovery, which on this occasion appeared to take place more quickly than the first attack some twelve years earlier. At some point around 1840, with Thomas back in work and possibly believing the worst was behind them, she convinced her husband they ought to move house. Their daughters were fast growing up and Matilda had reached an age were she could be sent out to work. In turn that meant more money for the household and increased wealth created greater opportunities to better their own lives. Space had become a serious problem and the small family needed more rooms in which to live. Thomas appeared not to have disagreed and so they moved into a house off St Peter's Street. Here they stayed without any recurrence of his illness until January of 1847.

St Peter's Street today. The author

The first signs that all was not well came during a conversation Thomas had with his friend of twenty years, Tom Boam. The two men had grown accustomed to spending time with each other after work so it had not been unusual for Tom to find that during the last week of January his friend arrived at his door perhaps a little more often than was the norm. What was unusual though was the fact that when pressed to give a reason for this sudden frequency of visits Thomas, whilst sharing a pipe of tobacco before the fire, had accused his wife of trying to poison him. Calmly he had talked of his fear that his own family had decided they wanted him dead. Tom unfortunately kept the conversation to himself. It was a serious error of judgement.

On 2 February, a few days after this fireside chat, Thomas's confused mind still in turmoil, he resolved to put an end to what he earnestly believed was his wife's murderous intent. At 2.30 pm he took a knife from the kitchen, walked calmly upstairs and stabbed her to death as she lay on the bed. Ann Cross stood no chance of fending off the attack but at some point did awake and scream for help. None came and, as

St Peter's Church. The author

she lay dying, her husband paced the bedroom floor waiting for night.

But the afternoon's events had not passed by totally unnoticed. Twelve-year-old Frederick Thumpstone worked in Brentall's bakery and confection shop. The shop yard backed onto the yard of a house owned by Joseph Osborne and his wife, landlord to the Cross family. At precisely the time Ann Cross had begun screaming he had been sent upstairs to the bakery that overlooked both yards to try and see what was going on. From his vantage point he could clearly see directly into the Cross's bedroom. At the time he peered out through the window, clearing away the condensation to obtain a better view, Ann Cross lay bleeding to death. But she lay beneath his line of sight and he could not see her. What he could see was her husband's agitated pacing of the room. After watching for several minutes and believing there was nothing untoward going on in the house, he returned to the shop with no story to tell.

At around a half past four that afternoon and with Thomas still walking the bedroom floor, Louisa, their youngest child arrived home. Without waiting for her father to come downstairs she made herself something to eat and as she sat at the table he joined her. The two ate in silence. After the meal and whilst clearing the table, Louisa asked her father why her mother had not come downstairs to join them. Thomas made up some excuse about her being ill. Suddenly concerned, Louisa said she would go up and see her before returning to her work. Realising his own daughter was about to discover her mother's murder Thomas grabbed a hold of her and, pushing her away from the stairs door, and blocked her path. The two struggled but for Louisa, only seventeen years old and slightly built, it was an uneven struggle. Distrusting her father, she ran from the house and returned with Mrs Osborne, the landlord's wife. She was made of sturdier stuff and made short work of pushing Thomas Cross away from the staircase and back into the kitchen. Louisa darted past the pair as they struggled and taking the stairs two at a time discovered the awful truth in the houses back bedroom. Shouting out in shock, she quickly ran back downstairs to confront her father but he was having none of it. Lunging at Mrs Osborne he stabbed her in the neck, Louisa screamed for help and grabbed a hold of the hand holding the knife to prevent him doing greater damage.

The screams were again heard in Brentall's shop but this time no one ran up to the bakery. William Waterfield, the oldest apprentice, ran across the cobbled yard and, scaling the partition wall, jumped into the Cross's yard and joined Louisa in trying to restrain her father. Other neighbours quickly joined the two, and within minutes he was disarmed and pinned to the ground.

At his eventual trial in Derby on 24 March he pleaded not guilty to murder and listened from his vantage point in the dock as the argument raged over his sanity or lack of it. Douglas Fox, surgeon to Derby Gaol, probably offered the court the most compelling evidence of insanity and was no doubt responsible for saving Thomas Cross from the scaffold. Twenty-four years as prison doctor and surgeon, he told the judge that it was this long medical background that gave him the knowledge to pronounce upon any man's sanity. Cross, he told the court, based upon this sound background, was clearly insane at the time he picked up the knife and murdered his wife. Describing his first meeting with his prisoner after his arrival at the prison, he was able to relate an in depth and detailed discussion the two men had held:

> *… He was in a very dejected, bewildered, and nervous state; I do not think he knew where he was; I could not make him enter upon the subject of the crime; I said, "Cross, you know where you are, do you not?" He looked about in a bewildered manner, and said no he did not. He afterwards said he thought he was at Spring Vale; and then again he*

seemed to doubt whether he was there; I felt convinced that he did not know where he was; I asked him if he had injured any person recently. He said he did not know that he had; I asked him if his wife was well, to which he replied that he was not aware that she was not, and that he did not know that she had been injured. I then asked him who were his neighbours: and he said he lived near the Osborn's and in answer to a question said he did not know Mrs Osborn had been injured. I then asked him pointedly whether he had stabbed her? He said no; the question had no visible effect upon his countenance; I found him with a quick pulse, a heated head, a restless eye, a loaded tongue, and very insane appearance of the countenance.

Mr Justice Patteson was convinced. Turning to the jury he instructed that they must return a verdict of not guilty to murder on the grounds of insanity, which they duly did and Thomas Cross returned to the Lunatic Asylum that ought never to have released him back to his family.

Chapter 6

A Strange Case of Poisoning – The Suspicious Death of Elizabeth Watson

1848

From the moment of her death the doctor suspected poisoning.

Twenty-four-year old Elizabeth Watson had been married for eighteen months and by March of 1848 was eight months pregnant with her second child. She and her husband were delighted at the prospect of an additional member to their family and had talked of having other children as the years went by. The marriage was solid and to all intents and purposes was successful and loving. A builder's labourer by trade working in Derby, her husband was absent throughout each day and had arranged for a nurse in the shape of local woman, Mrs Askew, to visit his wife on a daily basis. On Friday 5th, March Elizabeth began to vomit at regular intervals through the morning. Mrs Askew was called in to spend the day with her but in her experienced opinion the sickness was nothing out of the ordinary. Nevertheless, as a safeguard, her husband sent for his sister to spend the night with his wife. Full of cold himself and not wanting to pass the infection on he had already decided to sleep in a separate room and allow the two women to spend the night together. Elizabeth slept reasonably well and the sickness appeared to have passed.

The following day her husband John prepared breakfast at 6 am as his sister left for her work and husband and wife sat discussing the coming confinement. Perhaps understandably, Elizabeth was concerned that she would not survive the pregnancy and seemed a little despondent. She had apparently discussed the prospect of her death during the night with her sister in law, making mental lists of items she wished to pass to others if she died during her confinement. Despite the reassurances she was given in return regarding her continued good health, the feeling of dread had not left her by dawn.

The Cornmarket, Derby c1900. Author's collection

There was little her husband was able to say or do by way of reassurance but by the time he left for work he was content that he had at least alleviated some of her fears.

At around noon, the sickness of the previous day having apparently dissipated, she left the house and went visiting friends and neighbours. Mrs Askew met with her and made the final arrangements for nursing her through the final weeks of her pregnancy and bought groceries from a nearby shop. During the afternoon, obviously buoyed up by her returning health, she decided to take a long walk and enjoy what was left of the day. All was well until she arrived back at the house. Within an hour she was seized once more by dreadful stomach cramps and the vomiting began a second time. But now it had grown far worse than the previous day and calling for neighbours, she had someone fetch her husband home from work. When he arrived it was to find his wife in a state of almost total collapse. He ran to fetch local doctor, Mr Greaves, but he could not attend so sent medicines to ease the condition. By early evening Elizabeth Watson was dying. Dr Greaves arrived at the house at a little after 7 o'clock having been called a second time, but there was nothing he could do. She died shortly afterwards.

From the moment of her death the doctor suspected poisoning. All her symptoms led him to believe that she could not possibly have been suffering from any type of sickness that would have been associated with her pregnancy. Her demeanour throughout his visit, the manner in which she had died and the frequency of the vomiting attacks pointed him toward arsenic. A search of the house was made but revealed nothing. No empty medicine bottles, no hidden containers, and no powders. There was absolutely nothing to confirm that his suspicions had been well founded.

A post-mortem was therefore carried out on the following morning and analysis of the stomach contents confirmed unequivocally that she had either been given or had taken a large dose of arsenic. The lungs, heart, duodenum and stomach lining exhibited clear signs that her death had been as a result of poisoning, which had been administered over at least two days. Nothing

All Saints' church, Derby c1900 .
Author's collection

else in her physical makeup and that of her unborn child suggested she was anything other than healthy.

An inquest was opened at Derby Town Hall twenty-four hours later and analytical chemist, Albert Beranys, told the coroner that after closer examination of the samples taken from the dead woman's body he had been able to give a more definitive analysis of the poison that had caused her death. It was clear, he told the court, both arsenic and cacodyl (a stinking poisonous compound of arsenic, carbon and hydrogen) had been taken probably on more than one occasion but not over a prolonged period of time. This had induced vomiting, nausea, abdominal pain and diarrhoea. Nothing, he insisted, would have saved her life by the time Dr Greaves had arrived at the house; too much damage had already been done. The puzzle for the court was how and when. Investigations of all possible outlets for purchase of the

Irongate, Derby today. The author

poison had revealed absolutely nothing at all. A second thorough search of the house and the grounds around it had proved equally ineffective. The court was adjourned for a further twenty-four hours to allow more enquiries to be made further a field. Again it proved a fruitless quest.

As no evidence had been found to show that either the husband or the sister in law had administered the poison no charges were brought against them. Because on both occasions where clear signs of poison had been exhibited the woman had been alone, the coroner decided that it had to have been possible that she administered it herself. Accepting the fact that no supply of the arsenic had been found meant, in his opinion, there was insufficient evidence to show who by or how Elizabeth Watson had been brought to her death. The jury therefore returned a verdict that, the deceased died from the effects of arsenic, but how or by whom administered no evidence appeared to the jurors.

Chapter 7

With Malice Aforethought – The Murder of Phoebe Barnes

1851

Without a word and, as they watched, he then slit her throat from ear to ear.

Mrs Phoebe Barnes, a comfortably off widow, lived with her niece at Field House, Belper. The niece's husband, Reverend John Bannister, who lived with them, held the ministry for Belpers Bridge Hill church and, as would have been expected, was well known amongst the local community. The house itself was large, self-contained, standing within its own grounds and owned by the widow, as were a number of other properties and farms in the area. She employed a number of servants at the house and controlled all entry into her grounds by means of a gated road managed by a family who occupied what was commonly known as the lodge house, a small two-bedroom house situated at the bottom of a driveway approximately forty-five yards from the front door of the main house. Whether or not her wealth had been inherited or earned is unclear but without doubt it came from the ownership of these properties and the rents she was able to command. Some years earlier she had employed a local man, Anthony Turner, to act as her agent and

Church at the foot of Bridge Hill, Belper today. The author

Lane running between the church and what is thought to have been Field House.
The author

rent collector, setting him up in a house in the village. The appointment, possibly more an act of kindness rather than a rational business decision, had been unpopular but Turner had in his charge a young child. The child, a little girl, had been given up by Phoebe's brother. Just why the girl was abandoned by her father was never fully explained and Turner was himself initially reluctant to take on the role, but as the years passed he grew ever more paternal about the girl and began to see himself more and more as the father figure he was probably never intended to have become.

Phoebe Barnes, aware of his attachment to the child, did not share his view of blissful family life and his fatherly role. By Christmas of 1851 she had tired of what she saw as his unfriendly attitude toward her tenants. They had moaned and complained, as the months went by, that he was too heavy handed and often purposely difficult to deal with. Without a moment's hesitation or any apparent thought about the havoc she would cause, the widow of Field House wrote to her agent the day after Boxing Day:

Dec 27 1851

> *Mr Anthony Turner, Belper Lane End. Not being satisfied with your proceedings I do hereby give you notice that I have authorised and appointed Mr John Bridges to collect and receive my rents in your place and I do by this notice discharge you from collecting or receiving any more of my rents wheresoever or whatsoever from this twenty seventh day of Dec eighteen hundred and fifty one as witness my hand.*

Anthony Turner had been fired from his post, which meant not only loss of earnings but also loss of his house. The two were irrevocably tied together and the letter he received would, in his mind, destroy everything he had spent so much time building.

Within hours of its receipt he called at the chemist and grocer shop owned by good friend John Haslam. Buoyed by drink, he sat himself by Haslam's fire and handed the damning letter to the shopkeeper and his wife. They read it with equal incredulity but after several minutes discussing its lack of merit, could offer nothing by way of solace or advice. But Turner was not about to allow himself to be thrown out of his house and home. Suddenly snatching a knife from the shops counter he told the Haslams , 'I think I shall do something to be talked of', and stormed out into the street. There was a vehemence in the man's voice that John Haslam had never encountered before; a vehemence that he knew would be brought to bear on Phoebe Barnes. Leaving his shop he ran after Turner but was too far behind to catch him. By the time he arrived at the lodge Turner was already inside Field House.

Harriet Storer, cook to the Barnes household and the woman who had delivered the fateful letter, opened the door to him at a little after 8 pm. She saw that he was a little worse for wear through drink but deemed it safe enough to let him into the house. He told her in as calm a fashion as he was able that he wanted to speak to Mrs Barnes. The cook, concerned about his apparent drunkenness, nevertheless agreed to take his request upstairs. However, when she told Phoebe Barnes that her rent collector was downstairs she added the rider that in her opinion he was best sent away and allowed back when he was a little more sober. Mrs Barnes took no persuading and readily agreed, locking her door behind the cook as she left. But both had underestimated Anthony Turner. He was not about to be deflected from the confrontation he had set out to achieve and, before the cook had finished telling him he had to leave, she found herself on the floor and Turner heading for the stairs. Familiar with the layout of the house he knew exactly where to find his employer and, despite the locked door, managed to break his way into her rooms.

View of Belper today. The author

Harriet roused the household and Reverend Bannister and his wife ran upstairs to try and stop Turner attacking Mrs Barnes but were too late. As they burst into the bedroom, they saw she was being held down in a chair, secured by Turner's knee on her chest. Without a word and, as they watched, he then slit her throat from ear to ear. There followed a moment of shock during which both stood in disbelieving horror. Then, suddenly

Belper Lane End c1900. www.picturethepast.org.uk reproduced with kind permission of Mr Huskinson

Belper Lane End today. The author

galvanised into action, the Reverend lunged at Turner and in a brief struggle managed to grab a hold of his collar and wrench him away. The unfortunate Mrs Barnes, however, was already dead.

On 12 March 1852 Anthony Turner stood in the dock before Mr Justice Maule and pleaded not guilty to murder. The courtroom was packed with every seat taken and many people standing around the walls. Crowds had been gathering since dawn to get into the courthouse, such was the interest aroused throughout the whole of Derbyshire. Oblivious to the interest he had aroused Turner stood dispassionately at the heart of the court and watched the melodrama that was to be his life or death, play out before him.

Defended by a Mr W H Adams there was only one available defence that could legitimately be presented to the jury. If the prisoner at the bar was to be saved then he had to be proven either insane or to have acted irrationally, without malice aforethought, which would enable the twelve men and true to return a manslaughter verdict. Insanity he decided at an early stage would carry little weight. No medical testimony supported the notion and there had been no history of mental illness in the Turner family. So Mr Adams took the view that the killing had not been intended when Anthony Turner burst into Phoebe Barnes bedroom. Drunk, and seething with anger at having been dismissed from his post, he wanted the opportunity of confronting the woman he knew to be responsible. Murder had never been his intention, argued the defence barrister. Drink had been used as a palliative to his mental misery and had numbed his senses to such an extent that when he broke down her door and forced his way into her room, he was unable to see or think just what he was about. It was his guardianship of the young child in his care that had driven him to act as he did. Phoebe Barnes had deprived him of the means of providing the necessities this young girl would require over the coming years and, because the Barnes family were responsible for her very existence then they, as a family, were responsible for her maintenance through his employment. Being unprepared for the humiliation of being fired from his job had, momentarily, affected his mind. For this singular reason the idea of malice could not be a consideration:

> *The idea of malice being entertained by a man in such a frame of mind ...was absurd. The man did not know what he was doing, and consequently could have no malice; yet without malice, the crime of murder, cold blooded and deliberate murder, could not be committed.*

It was a powerful argument and, had Mr Justice Maule found sympathy with such a defence, then perhaps Anthony Turner would have found his predicament somewhat eased. But the learned judge knew well enough that the defence founded on the rocks of known fact. The prisoner, he told the jury, had deliberately taken a knife from the Haslam's shop, taken it with him to the Barnes household and had there used it to commit a murder. The notion that malice did not exist was nonsense. In his instruction to the jurors he told them pointedly that malice did not necessarily imply a deliberately formed and long cherished desire to cause death:

> *If a person performs an act with the intention of causing a serious mischief that constitutes malice; and if that intention of producing serious mischief causes death, that constitutes murder. If a quarrel and a struggle take place in a room, between two men, where there may be arms, and where they may be unpremeditatedly used, and death ensue to one of them, that may be a case of manslaughter; but here, in the case of an elderly lady, who is attacked in her own house, by a man who carries a knife with him, he (the learned judge) confessed he could see no circumstance, which could enable the jury to look on it as a case of manslaughter...*

It was a point of view that carried the day, despite the defence barrister's eloquent speech to the court and the observation of key witnesses, those that had seen the killing. The judge's destruction of his argument carried the greater weight with the jury and their verdict of Guilty was almost inevitable.

On Friday - 26 March, Anthony Turner mounted the steps to the scaffold three minutes after midday before a crowd of several thousand people. Numbered amongst this hoard of onlookers, according to the *Derby Mercury*, were large groups of mechanics and labourers. Timing their arrival to coincide with the start of proceedings they then sat in chattering groups eating their lunch of sandwiches as Calcraft, the executioner, pinioned the condemned man by the legs and arms before placing him above the trap. A huge cheer went up as the bolt was drawn and Turner was finally launched into eternity.

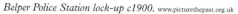

Belper Police Station lock-up c1900. www.picturethepast.org.uk

Chapter 8

For the Sake of an Inheritance – The Murder of Joseph Smith 1861

...there was a silence...followed by a single shot.

When Joseph Smith's wife died leaving him with four children to bring up, he resolved to free himself from all financial pressure. A shoemaker by trade, he had built up a profitable business over the years. Using some of the profit he had carefully nurtured, he bought a row of four houses in Ilkeston. Taking his family to live in one of these, he rented out the remainder and increased his income by the value of his rents. By 1861, some seven years later, his daughter Sarah had married and taken over one of the tenancies, his eldest son George had become employed in Nottingham's lace industry and his two youngest boys, Henry and Edward, by this time seventeen and thirteen respectively, had begun to learn the shoe trade. He and the three boys, who all lived under the same roof, lived well though Joseph was a careful man where money was concerned and none would ever have said they were any more than comfortable in their lifestyle.

On the surface then, at least as it appeared to those outside, the family's future was secured. But the Smith household was far from being perfect. Like many other families before and since, an underlying current of bitterness and resentment existed within the tight-knit little group, led in the main by George, the son whose greater age had allowed him more latitude and freedom than the others. He had no time for his father's occupation and had purposely chosen to work in Nottingham where he would be away from the house for much of every day, often not returning home at all or not until the early hours of the morning. This had angered Joseph, perhaps as it had been intended to do, and led inevitably to arguments. These in turn had become threats whereby George had been told that unless his behaviour changed he would find the house locked against him. It made little difference. George seemed to enjoy living his life on the edge, taking chances, breaking the rules and generally ignoring the

Ilkeston Railway Station c1910. www.picturethepast.org.uk

Ilkeston railway station site as it looks today. The author

tenet of his upbringing.

In April 1861 his father discovered that he had been involved in a number of different relationships with a variety of women from around the county and one of these, Ellen Cox, had apparently told him that she was pregnant. This led to ever-greater conflict within the house and a worsening of their relationship. But George was not about to move out. If there was one thing his father held that he coveted above all else, it was money. Joseph held a bank account at the Nottingham Savings Bank. George decided he was to have some of it.

On 1 May he stole the bankbook from a downstairs bureau. Then he and long time friend Henry Davis, a fellow lace worker, travelled by train into Nottingham where, after asking for directions, he eventually presented himself at the bank. Unfortunately for him he had underestimated the ease by which withdrawals could be made. The bank refused him, telling him that if he wished to take cash from his father's account then he must have a letter of permission. Thwarted but undaunted he then took the bankbook to a wine and spirit shop owned by a man named John Bridger. He explained to the shopkeeper that he had travelled from Ilkeston and wanted the loan of £1 to secure his rail ticket home, for which he would leave the savings book as surety, and that he would repay at the end of the week. A quick glance at the book balance of £200 convinced Bridger that his pound would be safe and the loan was made. Taking his £1 he then walked around Nottingham where he bought a pair of boots and at some point managed or contrived to lose his friend for a brief period during which he purchased a gun from *Webster, The Gun Shop* on Clumber Street. The two men eventually arrived back at Ilkeston railway station at around 7.30 pm.

Telling Henry, his shopping companion, that he had no wish to return home at that point, he asked if he would take the shoes back to his father's house for him. Henry agreed and the two parted. Within minutes George then met with Reuben Davis, another lace maker, and they walked the short distance to the *Queen's Head* where he later claimed they stayed until around midnight.

Meanwhile, back at home, Joseph had discovered the loss of his savings book and knew instantly just who had taken it. After finishing work at around half past seven he left the house, made several calls, the last one at his brother's house at nine o'clock. During this round of visits he had discovered that George had been in Nottingham for most of the day. Who said what and to whom is not known but certainly enough was said to arouse suspicion in Joseph's mind. The thought planted was simple enough. Distrustful of his eldest son, he began to speculate that if George had taken a train into the city then it had to have been for a reason and that had to have something to do with money. Joseph knew the only access to money in Nottingham would be through his own savings bank and, aware that his son had no savings, that money must have been his own. Confirmation of his son's dishonesty came after arriving home and carrying out a second fruitless search for the bank book.

After sending the two youngest sons to bed he sat in the main room of the house beside an open fire, dozed a while on the sofa and waited. George finally arrived home at a few minutes before midnight. In the argument that followed he denied having been in Nottingham, insisting he had never left Ilkeston and that he had not seen the bank book. Joseph was angry and accused his son of bringing scandal to the household. Moving the argument on he began to question him about Ellen Cox, the impending birth of her baby and other women he had heard George had involved himself with. The exchange of words became heated then, according to the two boys lying in their beds directly above them, then there was a silence, which lasted for about one minute followed by a single shot. Fearful for their lives the two boys jumped out of bed, pushed open the window and clambered onto the window sill screaming 'MURDER.' Without having seen anything the two were convinced that George had shot their father dead.

Sister Sarah, who lived next door, was the first on the scene. When she ran into the house there was no sign of George but her father lay on the floor before the fireplace clearly dead. He had been shot from close range in the left side of the head just behind the ear. She ran back out to bring in a neighbour and police were sent for. They arrived within minutes closely followed by the irascible George in a state of partial undress, no jacket on and no shoes on his feet. He insisted that his father had shot himself as he was about to undress for bed and that in a panic he had run to fetch Reuben Davis the man who, as he spoke, was standing behind him. The good friend agreed he had been brought from his bed after George had arrived at his house shouting of his father's suicide but said little else. Not satisfied and with the two younger boys now in the room accusing their elder brother of murder, police had only one question to ask. Where was the gun? If it had been suicide why did the weapon

The terraced area where the Smith's lived.
The author

used not lie beside the body or anywhere near it? A quick search had found nothing. They arrested George on suspicion and took him to Derby Gaol.

Once at the police station he told them he had taken the gun from the house after the shooting and had thrown it away as he ran to Reuben's house. Panic, he insisted, had clouded his judgement. According to his statement father and son had sat before the fire, one either side, arguing about George's lack of respect and generally bad conduct. At some point, he stated, Joseph had reached a hand into the oven, withdrawn a gun, held to his head and without any hesitation fired. He went on to say that his father had been exhibiting suicidal tendencies for some weeks, adding that only the day before in a letter written to Ellen Cox, the woman he intended to marry, he had told her that he expected his father to kill himself.

None of it was believed by the investigating police officers. They had concluded from the moment that they had arrested the man that suicide was total fabrication. Carefully, over the next twenty-four hours, they pieced together George's movements. Nottingham police checked out the shops and areas Henry Davis told them the two men had visited on their day out. Bridger's wine merchants confirmed the loan of the £1 against surety of the savings account, the bank confirmed his attempt to withdraw money from his father's account and after the gun had been discovered near to Reuben's house they traced the gun shop. David Webster confirmed that he had sold the gun and identified the purchaser as George Smith.

The inquest opened on 2 May at the *Queen's Head* at Ilkeston. Surgeon Mr G B Norman told the coroner that having carried out a post-mortem examination of Joseph Smith he was able to confirm that

Dewdrop Inn, *believed to have once been the* Queen's Head. The author

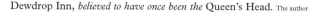

he had been shot from very close quarters, the wound being just behind the left ear and that the gun had been held pointing slightly downward because of the pattern of shot, which had travelled down into the brain not across it. Furthermore, the dead man had no blood staining to his hands yet the blood loss was quite large. In the doctor's opinion it would have been impossible for Joseph Smith to shoot himself in the head holding the gun at a downward angle and then not had the firing hand splattered by blood. The man, he told the court, had been murdered.

A variety of other witnesses testified to George's movements on the day of the killing, his involvement with a number of young women, his difficult relationship with his father, lack of money and the fact that he liked a drink. Perhaps more damning was the revelation that over the weeks leading up to the death of his father he told any that would listen that the man was going mad. He had spread the notion that he fully expected that he would take his own life. Yet no one, certainly not his own family, was able to corroborate this mental decline. No doctor was able to tell the court that there was any substance to George's implied threat and none of those close to him through his work had ever seen any sign of depression. The coroner returned a verdict of wilful murder against George Smith and, despite his continued insistence that he had not committed murder, he was sent for trial.

The case opened on 29 July. Crowds had been gathering since 7 am such was the interest generated across Derbyshire. When the Judge took his seat at nine o'clock there was not a seat to be had at any vantage point in the courtroom. George Smith, still resolute in his insistence that he was innocent, took his place in the dock. He was pale, drawn but apparently calm. After requesting that he hear each juror in turn announce their name and where they lived the case began.

Defended by a two man team of a Mr O'Brien and Mr Stephen, George Smith was determined to prove himself innocent of the charge and had pleaded not guilty in a strong, clear voice. Unfortunately for them all there was little that came out from the witness evidence to support the plea. After listening to the same witnesses that had testified at the inquest as to George's movements, none of which was particularly damning, the case began to turn markedly against them. Dr George Norman, who had carried out the original post-mortem, had been able to conduct a further and more thorough investigation of the body. After outlining once again the manner of the shooting and location of the wound he told the court that in total thirty-one pieces of shot had been removed from the brain. Most of that had come from the base of the skull and was corn shot.

A COPY OF VERSES ON THE

Murder of Joseph Smith

BY HIS OWN SON, AT ILKESTON, MAY 2, 1861.

A dreadful deed of murder to you I will unfold,
'Tis a tale as sad and horrid as ever yet was told;
At Ilkeston in Derbyshire, alas, it is too true—
A wretched son the deed has done—his own dear
father slew.

    His own dear father he did slay,
    On Wednesday eve, the first of May.

George Smith, a sad and wretched man, his father's
blood did spill,
On that fatal spot, he fired the shot which did his
father kill.
It is supposed he meant to rob his parent of his
wealth
And when the deed was done he said his father
killed himself.

His wedding day was drawing near—he did pre-
meditate
That his father and himself should meet with an un-
timely fate—
The fatal murderous weapon he grasped in his hand,
And fired on his father dear, as we can understand.

To see his brothers, Henry and Edwin standing by,
Praying o'er their murdered father, tears falling
from each eye,
Would almost pierce a heart of steel to see how they
did weep
O'er their mangled, murder'd father, who in death's
cold arms did sleep.

Their brother George to murder him with Satan
had engaged—
The son who shot his father is but twenty years of
age:
Now lying in a gaol, and pond'ring o'er the deed
he done—
Reflecting on the murder of a father by his son.

Oh, list you tender parents and all you sons likewise!
This cannot fail to draw a tear from every human
eye.
Whatever could possess him such a dreadful deed
to do,
When on Wednesday night, the first of May I is
own kind father slew.

He now his trial does await, approaching is the time,
His dear unhappy parent was aged forty-nine—
Murder'd in the prime of life, oh, awful tragedy,
By one whom he fondly cherished and dandled on
his knee.

The dear and younger children when they their
father saw,
The agony they did endure, they on their knees did
fall,
While tears fell from their weeping eyes in torrents
on the floor,
Crying, "Our dearest father on earth we'll see no
more.

Oh, children be dutiful unto your parents kind,
The good advice they give you bear always in your
mind.
There is one above who watches you throughout the
night and day—
Then think upon the wretched youth who did his
father slay.

    At Ilkeston they were known well,
    Where they many happy years did dwell.

(Copyright).

C. LANCASTER, PRINTER, LEEDS.

Pamphlet of the murder of Joseph Smith. Derby Local Studies Library

The wound, in his opinion, had been caused by the weapon being discharged from above the deceased's head. It had been fired from the left side and, had it been suicide, would have had to have been fired by Smith using his left hand. Dr Norman had been his doctor for many years and knew that Smith was not left-handed. The brother, Samuel Smith, further corroborated this and other experts who added testimony to the effect that trying to fire a gun at such close quarters whilst holding it in the hand that was rarely used would, in all probability, have resulted in a totally different type of wound.

Further compelling evidence was produced in the form of an extract from a short letter written by George Smith to Ellen Cox:

My Dear – I told my father this morning [day before the shooting] *and he is like a madman and I do believe he will make away with himself…*

The woman he was to have married and the mother of his expected child had been told, argued the prosecution, that a death was expected, that the father Joseph was likely to take his own life. In other words George was paving the way for a suicide bid, which he also knew would leave him as the eldest son inheriting the whole of the family estate. The jury were told that no will existed and George believed that under those circumstances the eldest son always succeeded the father. The defence team insisted this could not have been the case. The letter was not an indicator of their client's guilt simply because he raised the prospect of his own father's demise. But the damage had been done. When little Martha Cockayce took the stand toward the end of the afternoon and told the court that at 8 pm on the night of the killing George Smith had asked her to buy for him a pennyworth of shot corn No 2 from a man called Isaac Gregory, which she did, there was no going back.

In his final submission the defence barrister, Mr O'Brien, told the jury that despite all the evidence to the contrary the whole case rested upon a chain of circumstantial evidence. George Smith, he argued, had told the truth when he raised the question of his father's sanity amongst friends because no witness brought to court had agreed with that fact was irrelevant, not everyone would have been aware of the man's mental stability or lack of it, particularly if they had not seen him on a regular basis. The gun, whilst obviously the weapon used, was not proven to have been fired by the prisoner though he accepted it had been purchased by him and furthermore no-one could, with absolute certainty, say that the deceased man, right handed or not, could not have fired the fatal shot regardless of the gun's rightful ownership. If, he argued, George Smith had murdered his father why did he do it in a state of undress and why not at some other time?

The Confession of Geo. Smith, to the Governor, of Derby Gaol, who is to be Executed on Friday August 16th, 1861.

You feeling Christian pray attend,
  And listen unto me,
While unto you I will unfold,
  This dreadful tragedy ;
Committed by a guilty one,
  As you shall quickly hear,
Upon his father at Ilkeston,
  Well known in Derbyshire.

CHORUS—Oh ! the dreadful deed was done,
  A father murdered by a son.

I hope you will a warning take,
  By what I now relate,
And think on my untimely end,
  For wretched is my fate ;
I might have lived in happiness,
  As you shall quickly hear,
All with my aged father,
  At Ilkeston, in Derbyshire.

Sure satan must have tempted me,
  Upon that fatal day,
My kind and tender Father,
  To take his life away ;
All with a deadly weapon,
  It was my full intent,
I gave him not the shortest time,
  On earth for to repent.

I was confined in Derby gaol,
  My trial to await,
For the awful crime of murder,
  My sufferings were so great.

The jury found me guilty,
  And I am condemned to die,
An awful death of public scorn,
  Upon the gallows high.

The black cap being in readiness,
  When I was tried and cast,
The learned judge with solemn voice,
  The awful sentence passed ;
You must prepare to meet your God,
  We can no mercy show
So pray for mercy from above,
  For none is here below.

I dread to think upon the hour,
  All on that fatal morn,
When I must ascend the scaffold high,
  To die a death of scorn,
To the fatal spot thousands will come,
  That dreadful sight to see,
George Smith to end his days,
  Upon the gallow tree.

I have brought disgrace upon myself,
  My friends and family,
No one I'm sure will sympathize
  Or soothe my misery,
I must prepare to meet my God,
  I hear the solemn knell,
My time is come I must away,
  Farewell, a last farewell.

T. & W. PLANT, PRINTERS, 32, CLARE STREET, NOTTINGHAM.   TRAVELLERS SUPPLIED.

Broadsheet confession of George Smith. Derby Local Studies Library

They were key points and possibly found their mark amongst some of the jurors but when the judge raised the issue of money, reminding them that the son had stolen the father's savings book, that he had attempted to steal money from the account, that he had purchased a gun when no guns were ever used by the family and that he had enquired as to his rights of inheritance, the case was lost. They returned after a short adjournment with a verdict of Guilty.

As the uproar in court subsided George Smith jumped up on the chair in the dock and addressed his peers:

> *Hear me, gentlemen, state the facts of the case. I did buy the pistol, the caps and the powder, and I took it into the house. I did not leave it in the first time, but I left it in the drawer when my father lay on the right hand side of the sofa, but I could not say whether he saw me or not…I put the remaining shot in the pigsty in the yard…My father sat in this position* [indicating the fireplace], *but I cannot say if he was smoking or not, and he picked something up and putting up his left hand shot himself. As I was going down to Reuben Davis's with my right hand I flung it away…Pass sentence over me, but I am (turning to the crowd) an Englishman, I will face it…I am innocent and I stand here with a clear conscience…*

The judge, deeply angered and affected by the outburst, told George Smith in no uncertain terms that in his opinion the correct verdict had been returned:

> *…That is not the statement of a man feeling concerned for the death of his father. It is in the spirit of bravado from a heart not full of regret for the dreadful affair, and placed under the dread accusation you have stood under, but rather one who, addresses the people in the court with a heart that has been steeled by sin, and let me ask whether it is likely that you could stand there and so conduct yourself if you had not a guilty conscience. I do not think you could have done so unless your heart had been hardened by a course of sinfulness, the last act of which was that you might gain your father's property by shedding his blood…*

Stung by the judge's retort, he clambered down from his vaulted position above the crowded courtroom and said no more. For the next three weeks there was fevered speculation as to his guilt or innocence with newspapers adding their own views of the murder. For his part George Smith said nothing more until 15 August, twenty-four hours, prior to his execution. Claiming he had been so well attended by the Ilkeston's prison chaplain and giving that fact as his reason for reconsidering his position, he made a full confession. So when he stepped out in front of the huge Derby crowds to be pinioned by William Calcraft and walked to the trap he did so with perhaps a clear conscience.

Chapter 9

The Love of a Jealous Man – The Murder of Eliza Morrow

1862

Neighbours ran out as they heard her scream...

When Eliza Morrow moved in to No 4 Court Agard Street in March 1859 it was meant to have been the start of a new life. Moving with her, was Ann Webster, who was to share the house and pay rent for a room on the second floor. Employed as a mill-hand, Eliza had managed to remain self sufficient, her wage of seven shillings and sixpence (37.5p) just about paid for all she needed and if she was short there were plenty of willing neighbours who would step in and help. The court itself was no more than a yard hemmed in by houses and therefore well populated, which meant that privacy was at a premium, at times a godsend at other times a cause of anger and frustration. Those living nearest shared your space and as a consequence shared a large part of your life and what they did not see their children did. But it was a life Eliza had grown used to. As long as the money kept coming in, it was also a lifestyle she could cope with. But all that was about to change.

Just before Christmas 1861 the mill began to struggle for new orders and the workforce was put onto short time. It was possibly Eliza's first experience of living below what she would have regarded as subsistence level. The cut backs meant her take home pay fell to five shillings and four pence (27p). Life took a distinct downward turn and suddenly she found herself struggling to buy food and pay her rent. Falling short by more than two shillings, this began to put severe restrictions around her life and at times meant that she had no money by the middle of the week. Christmas would have been particularly hard had not she been able to borrow money. The man that stepped into her life and made the loan, Richard Thorley, had been only too willing to help.

He had known Eliza for some five months, had become infatuated with her and wanted to build a relationship. Loaning the money was meant to enhance his prospects, which for a time it did, as did the potatoes and rabbits he provided through the Christmas week and in the early part of the New Year. The two began a relationship of sorts. Kept at arms length to some extent, Eliza allowed him to call, which he began to do every night of the week, but she was careful not to allow him to move in with her. His became a familiar face around the court but there was a darker side to his character. Richard Thorley's obsession with Eliza brought with it a level of jealousy she had never encountered before. To him she was all that mattered in his life and he believed it perfectly rational to expect her to reciprocate, which meant she must exclude all other men.

In January 1862 she discovered exactly what that actually meant. Seeing her talking to a young man in the street, minutes away from where she lived, his jealousy boiled over. Breaking up the conversation he dragged her away and beat her severely. Bruised, eyes blacked and in some discomfort she managed to get herself home where a shocked Ann Webster begged her to call in the police and have him arrested. She refused but from that point on refused to have any more to do with the man. But Thorley was persistent, the calls continued and undeterred by Eliza's refusal to forgive his violent outburst he succeeded in at least re-establishing his foothold in her life, though not to the degree it had once been. They were civil with each other but not much more and for obvious reasons she became a little wary when around him.

At some point at the end of January or early February, some four weeks or so after being attacked, she had begun to meet with a soldier. There was nothing to suggest it was ever anything serious or ever could have been and the meetings were not on a regular basis but the ever-present Thorley was quick to notice. Police had been called to the house on 12 February after Thorley had attempted to force his way through the back door, ostensibly only to give her some sausages because he knew she was still struggling for money. They did not believe him but made no arrest. He received a warning about his future conduct. For Eliza it was all too little and far too late. On the following evening, still consumed by jealousy, he accosted her in the middle of the courtyard. There followed an argument witnessed by lodger Ann Webster, which resulted in him grabbing Eliza around the neck, dragging her toward the wall at the top of the yard and with a blunt cut-throat razor cutting her throat. Neighbours ran out as they heard her scream and clearly saw the two of them fall to the ground. Thorley quickly picked himself up and ran away. Eliza was carried, still alive, into her house. Joseph German, surgeon, arrived fifteen minutes later

Ye Olde Spa Inn *today.* The author

to find her still breathing having been cut in three separate places. There was nothing he could do and she died as he tried to stem the bleeding.

Police arrested Thorley shortly after he left the *Spa Inn*, Abbey Street where he had arrived within minutes of the killing, smeared in blood and exhibiting a severely cut right hand. Thorley told anyone that would listen that he had been fighting with an Irish gang in the pub down the road, the *Abbey Inn*, which had resulted in his hand being slashed by a broken glass. Known by the landlord, Tom Chapman, the notion of being in a fight with Irish workers was not uncommon, neither was trouble at the *Abbey Inn*, so he was easily believed. Serving him with ginger beer and rum, he watched as the bloody handkerchief was removed from his hand and the open wound exhibited for all to see. The cut was severe and still bleeding when Thorley walked back out on to the street.

Detective Sergeant Thomas Vesey, who knew him well, made the final arrest. There was no struggle and after being taken into the *New Inn* by the policeman, Thorley freely admitted that he had attacked Eliza. The sergeant told him she was dead and Thorley apologised.

The Abbey Inn *c1950*. www.picturethepast.org.uk

Once at Derby Police Station he again admitted his guilt and told the officers he had killed her because he believed she had paid too much attention to a young soldier and not to him.

The trial opened 0n 24 March 1862 before Mr Justice Williams and a packed courtroom. In a hesitating but clear voice Richard Thorley pleaded not guilty to murder. From the outset it was always going to be difficult for him, or rather his defence barrister, to convince the court that murder had not been intended. He had been seen with the dead woman, had a record of abusing her and too many people saw the killing take place. Notwithstanding all that, he had confessed his guilt after being arrested. As he stood in the dock on that cold March day he must have realised the futility of his defence. But there was no

Abbey Street today. The author

alternative. If he was to escape the gallows in the face of such overwhelming evidence then it could only be on the grounds of manslaughter.

The two-man defence team of Mr Pickering and Mr Yeatman certainly intended that to be the case and after listening to various eyewitness accounts of that night's event, none of which could be disputed, it was left to Mr Yeatman to address the jury. In an impassioned plea he argued that though there could be no doubt that it had been Thorley who had killed Eliza Morrow it had not been premeditated:

> ...*In returning a verdict of wilful murder they* [the jury] *must be satisfied that the prisoner slew the deceased with malice aforethought.*

This, he felt strongly had not been proved. He told the jurors that the number of wounds inflicted, three cuts to the throat, had been a clear indicator of his state of mind. To have killed her in this way, he argued, showed that he had not acted coolly or deliberately rather that he had been impassioned to the point of frenzy. There was no premeditation; therefore, murder could not be a legitimate charge to level and only

Agard Street today. The author

manslaughter fitted the circumstances of the crime:

> *There could be no doubt that he loved her better than his life, and that she had a similar attachment for him, not all the persuasions of* [Ann] *Webster could induce* [Eliza] *Morrow to turn him off.*

The second point was debatable but the suggestion that this had been a killing borne out of love was no doubt a valid conclusion and one which, possibly, he hoped the jury would seize upon, particularly when he added that because of this deeply felt love, jealousy, the motive cited by the prosecution, was almost justified.

It certainly was a valiant attempt to lessen the penalty and possibly held sway amongst many in the courtroom, a packed arena of spectators that had sat in silence throughout the address. But it had no impression upon the jury. After a short deliberation they returned the expected verdict and Richard Thorley was sentenced to death.

Whilst languishing in the condemned cell he showed no remorse and when asked to make an act of contrition, he refused, telling the

REFLECTIONS

UPON THE UNTIMELY END OF

ELIZA MORROW

AND THE AWFUL FATE OF

RICHARD THORLEY.

Richard Thorley was hanged at Derby, Friday, April 11th, 1862, for the Wilful Murder of Eliza Morrow, on Thursday, February 13th, 1862, to whom he was paying his addresses, but which she had latterly desired to be discontinued.

Young men and maidens! list, I pray,
   To what I'm going to preach;
And when you've heard me, do not say,
   " Stern facts can never teach."

Poor Richard Thorley's dead, and gone
   Into another world;
Then let not vengeful thoughts upon
   His mis-spent life be hurl'd.

Much good he had within his mind,
   For all its rough outside;
To wife and mother truly kind,
   As to his destin'd bride.

And though his faults were very great,
   There's some excuse for all,
Which formed his manhood's fatal state,
   And brought his dreadful fall.

No father's arm, of lawful power,
   Control'd his ripening age,
Till habits, formed from hour to hour,
   Should make his manhood sage.

Thoughtless and gay, he joined the ring,
   Round mirth and ribald laughter,

With those, who to the wild waves fling,
   All thoughts of an hereafter.

And one he woo'd in honest heart,
   And lov'd but to his sorrow,
Smil'd as she barb'd the poison'd dart—
   Poor lost Eliza Morrow.

How little could her silly pride
   Foresee so sad an end,
Or sure she would have gently tried
   That erring soul to mend.

Better than taunt or cruel jeer,
   Had been that purpose, wise—
Love might have chang'd his mad career,
   But *now, a felon dies!*

O! woman! let not vain desires
   Your tender bosoms stir,
For ah! these dark infernal fires
   Have made a murderer.

Be to your nature nobly true,
   In feeling and behaviour;
Till God in you, shall form anew,
   Mans' help-meet, guide, and saviour.

BY A LADY.

L. BROOKES, PRINTER, DERBY.

Broadsheet poem of Eliza Morrows murder. Derby Local Studies Library prison chaplain that he had nothing to apologise for:

...Why should I feel sorry? She deserved what she got.

At 2 am on Friday 11 April he sat and wrote out a full and frank confession to the murder. In it he tried to explain the nature of the relationship he and Eliza had shared. Clearly stormy and for her part perhaps reluctant at times, there was no doubting the depth of his feelings, nor could he disguise the jealousy that eventually drove him to kill her. Later that same day he walked calmly to the scaffold and paid the ultimate price.

Chapter 10

The Sword Stick Killing – The Murder of Sarah Potter

1864

Blood had spilled out from the narrow wound and pooled across the bedroom floor.

James Potter was described by those who knew him as being a morose man, a man prone to making mistakes, often forgetful, argumentative and of peculiar habits. Just what those habits were is not known but they cost him his job of three years, working for Derby's sheriff's office. Out of work, he resorted to drink and as a consequence of that he began beating his wife Sarah. Aged fifty-five, she ought to have left him behind and moved on, as the police had told her to do on many occasions. But changing life at that age and in the Derby of 1864 was not going to be easy and Sarah had no intentions of trying.

On 22 December that same year she turned up at the door of local police inspector Edward Green at a little after 9 pm and pleaded with him to have her husband committed to an asylum. She had been beaten but not seriously injured. Powerless to help Green he listened to what the woman had to say but then had no choice other than to send her home. Concerned however, and all too well aware of the threat Potter posed, he knew there would be no sleep for him if he failed to organise some sort of watch on her house. So at 10 pm he met with local police sergeant, Thorpe, and after a brief discussion about Sarah's fear of her husband it was agreed that the sergeant would keep a close eye on the Potter's house during his night shift. Satisfied, he then made his way back home but before he could place his key in the lock of his door she was back, still distraught, still scared and by now very cold. Taking her to one side he explained to her what he had arranged and convinced her to return home. Realising at that point that there was little alternative, a reluctant Sarah did as she was told. But she knew that the rage that had been turned against her and had caused her to run away would not have been assuaged by the time she

Traffic Street today. The author

had made the long walk home. Jealousy was a deadly and desperate emotion and she knew that James Potter was never going to forgive what he saw as betrayal.

That betrayal, as he saw it, had been borne out of his belief that his wife was involved in an affair. The Potters had taken in a lodger, John Stone, earlier in the year. A married man whose wife worked at Derby Infirmary and who, because of the shifts worked by the two, both kept odd hours. The very fact that they rarely spent time with each other had created, in James Potter's mind at least, the opportunity for his wife to spend time alone with the man. She in turn had insisted there was no truth in the allegations but her denials just seemed to strengthen his belief. Over the weeks leading up to Christmas he had already beaten her several times just on the strength of them. So there was little doubt that her fears for returning back to the terraced house in Traffic Street were well founded.

According to Sarah's daughter, Elizabeth Clements, who lived a street away, her mother arrived back home at a round 11 pm. Her father, who had spent the period of her absence from the family home in the pub, followed her into the house within minutes. Intoxicated but not drunk he demanded his evening meal and Sarah, after setting it in front of him, left the house and walked to the pub her husband had vacated minutes earlier to fetch a jug of ale. Inexplicably angered he ran out after her, closely followed by the daughter and after catching her inside the public bar viciously attacked her. The fight was brief, the two being separated by Elizabeth with help from the landlord, after which they were ordered back out onto the street. Once there, a running battle of sorts took place as they walked back home with James finally refusing to allow the two women back into the house. He had the key, the door was locked and as far as he was concerned it was staying that way. He went off to *Bradbury's* public house where he stayed until police constable Lester arrived some half an hour later to force him back home. Stone, the lodger, had arrived after his long day shift to find himself locked out and two women freezing in the yard. He it was had insisted that Elizabeth find a policeman and get her father out of the pub. A reluctant James heeded the police warning about just what would happen if he refused. According to later testimony he appeared calm at that stage.

London Road today. The author

Daughter Elizabeth stayed at the house after the door had been unlocked, until she felt that her father was calm and that her mother would not be in danger of another beating. She finally left at around half past midnight. Everything seemed to have settled down. The arguments had ceased, John Stone had retired to bed and despite being asked by Sarah to spend the night downstairs Elizabeth felt it safe to leave her mother and father together. Locking the door behind her she made the short walk back to her own house.

At 1 am sergeant Thorpe found Potter standing, hands in pockets, at the corner of Traffic Street and London Road. The men spoke and the police sergeant told him to go back home. He refused and added that he would only go back if the sergeant went with him. He agreed and the two walked in silence the short distance to the Potter house. As they arrived in front of the house James said he had been locked out and had no way of gaining an entrance. Trying doors front and back, which were locked, the policeman told him he would have to clamber through a window. Luckily he managed to find a downstairs sash window unlocked. Easing it up he told a reluctant James to push himself in. He refused, said he would only enter if the sergeant went in

Corner of Traffic Street and London Road today. The author

with him. After some persuasion he agreed and, after helping James through the narrow opening, he followed on behind. Lighting a candle the policeman then followed a somewhat nervous James upstairs. Once on the short landing the two men stopped outside the bedroom door and, despite sergeant Thorpe's cajoling, Potter refused to enter. Taking him by the shoulders he gently pushed him through the door. As the candlelight swept across the room Sarah Potter could be clearly seen, partly covered by blankets, her eyes open and staring blankly at the ceiling. James Potter covered his eyes with both hands and from beneath the veil of fingers cried out, 'Dead, dead, dead.' Holding the candle above the bed the sergeant saw beneath the flickering light that she had been stabbed once beneath her left breast. Blood had spilled out from the narrow wound and pooled across the bedroom floor. After taking James Potter out of the room and into the street he stopped two women and sent them off to find a doctor. Additional policemen arrived with him. Once the doctor had certified Sarah dead, Potter was taken to Derby police station and charged with murder.

At the inquest it was shown that a walking stick sword had been used to stab her, the blade of which had penetrated her heart killing her instantly. Potter had apparently tried to hide the murder weapon behind a dresser in the bedroom but it had been easily found in daylight. As for time of death, it became clear after evidence from adjoining neighbours who had heard cries of murder that the killing had taken place at 12.30 am. Clearly, Elizabeth Clements' belief that her parents were safe to be left alone was ill founded. As she took the first steps along the streets to walk home her father had calmly murdered the mother, apparently without any provocation. The coroner returned a verdict of wilful murder.

At his trial on 9 March 1865, before Mr Justice Willes, James Potter pleaded not guilty. His defence barrister, Mr Fitzjames Stephen, told the jury that his client could not have murdered his wife had he been sane. The defence, with little else to aid them, embarked upon a course that would claim insanity had been the cause of his actions two days before Christmas, 1864. After hearing all the police evidence as to James Potter's movements on the night of the murder, including the discovery of Sarah's body and his eventual confession, they began to seriously question his mental health.

Two cases of mental illness had been registered in his family; an aunt and a grandmother had both been committed to asylum's some seven years earlier. This, claimed the defence, laid a clear and unequivocal foundation within the family of insanity. James, they argued, had also been affected but possibly it had never manifested itself in so violent a manner. In a speech for the defence that lasted for one hour and thirty-five minutes Mr Fitzjames Stephen told the jury there were only three questions to answer:

> *First, did Potter kill his wife?* [pointing to the prisoner] *Potter says No. Myself, no doubt he did. Second, did Potter know the nature and quality of the act he was doing? Thirdly, could he help it, had he entirely that control over his actions which you and I have, and which would render him responsible in the sight of God and amenable to the law of the land?*

He went on to question whether or not Potter had been able to resist the impulse to kill and whether or not he had true knowledge of just whom he was killing. Insanity claimed the defence, as shown through the family history, had already impacted upon the Potter household. Sarah Potter had been well aware of her husband's predilection towards madness. She had told the police, she had requested on the night of her death that he be locked away and that he was to her clearly mad. She had chosen to stay with him because she believed he would one day recover. Perhaps he garnished the truth a little here but no doubt the argument had merit.

Unfortunately for Mr Fitzjames Stephen, Derby's prison surgeon disagreed. He claimed in court that having had access to James Potter on a daily basis since his arrest, he had seen nothing to warrant the supposition that he had been insane at the time he ran his wife through with the walking stick blade. Familiar with the accused from his days as a surgeon at Derby Infirmary, apart from hesitancy in his manner there was nothing, he insisted, that had manifested itself any differently than it had when he had been a patient some years earlier. James Potter, claimed the surgeon, was a cunning and obstinate man. His refusal to enter the house with the policeman after being taken home were evidence of a man using that cunning to create the illusion of madness. The reason he had appeared perhaps vague about the killing was simply because to have behaved in any other way would inevitably have incriminated him. The prisoner, Dr Gisborne insisted, was not of unsound mind.

Undaunted, the defence brought a number of witnesses to the court each of whom testified to some mental decline in Potter over the months leading up to the murder. He had become forgetful, had been irritable and irrational when trying to make decisions and had exhibited signs that he was on the verge of some form of madness. But all these witnesses had no knowledge of the illness they discussed; all were laymen and as such should have had no real bearing on the outcome of the case. They did not and the jury, after a short deliberation, returned a guilty verdict and placing the black cap upon his head, Mr Justice Willes sentenced Potter to death.

On 22 March the conviction was overturned when it was decided to postpone the sentence for a period of seven days, which would allow two physicians to examine Potter in greater detail. The crowds that had turned up at Derby to witness the execution were turned away, disgruntled at being denied the opportunity of watching what they considered to have been nothing more that a common murderer mount the scaffold. On Saturday, 25 March James Potter was finally transferred to Broadmoor.

Chapter 11

A Strange Case of Drowning – The Suspicious Death of Lois Ann Taylor

1881

As he looked down from the high bank, her body slowly appeared.

When nineteen-year-old Lois Taylor left her parents home, *Gallows Inn*, Ilkeston, at 7 pm on Saturday, 19 November she told her mother that she expected to be home at the usual time. The usual time was around 9.30 pm but Mary Taylor knew that since her daughter had met up with a young man named Henry Pearson the usual time had often stretched to half past ten or eleven o'clock. She had no objection to the later hour and had always known that as Lois grew up she would push against the boundaries set by her parents. But this night was to be very different.

By midnight there was no sign of Lois. After sitting up until 2 am the worried parents had a restless night's sleep but convinced themselves that she had probably stayed over at Henry's house. His parents they knew and felt secure in the knowledge that this family would have found her a bed for the night and that she would return at some point on the Sunday morning. They were very wrong and after Lois had failed to arrive home by that evening they began to panic. November meant that the days were obviously shorter and as night fell they decided it would be better to wait for Monday and daylight before going out to try and locate her.

Mary Taylor was knocking on Henry Pearson's door by mid-morning but had to wait for him to return home from Hewitt's lace making factory before she could question him. When the two met he had little to say. According to him, the two had parted company on the Nottingham toll road at around midnight. There had been no argument but Lois, he insisted, had said that she was not returning home but was going away. Just where she had intended to go at that time of night he claimed not to know. Mary was not satisfied. She questioned him again, pushing the point that they must have argued

The Gallows Inn *prior to demolition c1960. Believed originally to have been a farmhouse.*
www.picturethepast.org.uk

and pointedly telling him that she did not believe his story. Lois, she knew, had taken no other clothes, and had appeared perfectly rational and normal. There could have been no way that she would have left home to travel without discussing it first with her own parents. She went to Ilkeston police.

Inspector Cowley listened to the mother's story and agreed that the behaviour she described did seem irrational. He began a door-to-door investigation, questioning the Ilkeston neighbourhood to try and ascertain whether or not anyone could verify Henry Pearson's version of events from the previous Saturday. He knew that the Nottingham road was constantly busy, as a main thoroughfare between the small town and the city, people walked the route at all times of day and night. It was therefore perfectly reasonable to find witnesses able to corroborate some or all of the young man's story. It proved far more difficult than he had envisaged at the outset. After two days no one had been found that could clearly identify the couple but what had begun to emerge was that sounds of raised voices and the screams of a woman had been heard at some point along the canalside at around 1 am.

Inspector Cowley took the unprecedented step of requesting the manager of the Erewash Canal to have the section of the waterway nearest to where the sound of those voices had been heard drained. Work began during Wednesday night, four days after Lois's disappearance. It yielded results at 7.30 am on the following Thursday. As he looked down from the high bank, her body slowly appeared lying on the muddy bottom of the canal basin. After arranging for it to be carefully carried to the *Horse and Jockey* public house he called in Dr Wood, the medical officer he had used to examine previous victims of suspicious deaths. A cursory examination revealed, perhaps as he had expected, that all was not as it should have been.

Lois had left home on the previous Saturday wearing a brown dress, black-jacket, black trimmed hat and a pink woollen necktie pinned over her shoulder. When she was found all these items of clothing were as described and intact but it was the necktie that caused the examining doctor to believe that the young woman had been murdered. Instead of being worn as Mary Taylor had described to the police it was found wrapped three times around her neck and knotted in two places beneath her chin. Other marks on her body indicated a level of violence consistent with Lois having been murdered. Death, he told Inspector Cowley, appeared to have been caused by strangulation.

Henry Pearson was immediately arrested and hauled up before Ilkeston's Colonel Newdigate, Chairman of the Bench. Despite several attempts during the course of the morning he had been unable to pinpoint exactly where on the Nottingham road the young couple had been on the Saturday of Lois's disappearance. This failure coupled with the certain knowledge that he had been in the woman's company until the early hours were sufficient to warrant a degree of suspicion against him. The good colonel agreed and had him remanded in custody.

On Friday morning the coroner, Mr Whiston, opened the inquest into the death at the *Horse and Jockey* whilst the body lay in an adjoining room. For many it was to have been an open and shut case. The woman had been found drowned, Henry Pearson could not give

The Gallows Inn *today.* The author

an accurate and believeable enough account as to his own involvement or movements on the night of her death, and she had all the hallmarks associated with having been murdered. There was a hush in the courtroom as Dr Ward took the stand.

Fortunately for Henry Pearson, who had spent an uncomfortable night in the cells, his evidence was to prove far more elucidating than he could ever have expected. Having had twenty-four hours to conduct a full post-mortem he had uncovered a series of facts that caused him some surprise. The marks found on her body after she had been lifted from the canal, the marks he believed had been caused violently, had disappeared. More astoundingly her lungs had been congested and swollen by water and the ligature marks around her neck had simply faded away. Lois Taylor, he told a shocked court, had actually drowned. She could not have been strangled to death, as he had earlier believed though there was the distinct possibility that she could have been attacked and pushed into the water whilst still alive. Only one thing, according to his testimony, cast doubt upon the notion of violence being used upon her and that one single fact was that she had removed her earrings. Would she have done so had she been attacked by her lover?

The court was thrown into some confusion. The lover, Henry Pearson, had been, at the very least, somewhat evasive under questioning. Screams or at least loud voices had been heard around the bank side where she had been found, a ligature of sorts appeared to have been placed around her neck and there had been no evidence found to show that at the time of her death she was in any way mentally unbalanced. But to have drowned meant that there was sufficient doubt cast upon Pearson's involvement in her death, if indeed there had been any.

Was she pushed or did she jump? No one was ever to discover the truth.

The Erewash Canal where Lois Taylor drowned. The author

Chapter 12

A Case of Starvation – The Killing of Baby Annie

1889

The hair was clotted together and the nightgown was nearly black.

our-month-old Annie Ada Martin had the great misfortune to have been born into a household where alcohol meant more than money. When her father James Martin realised that his wife was pregnant he decided to take work at his mother-in-law's drapery shop in Derby, but only for two days a week. The intention was to bring some money into the household that could be used to help feed the child. It is doubtful if any of that money ever got anywhere near his daughter. Within a month of Annie's birth

The River Derwent at Derby c1900. Author's collection

neighbours began to notice that the child was wasting away, her arms had grown extremely thin, she had no colour about the face and constantly cried. Not that this situation seemed to have any effect on either parent.

Sarah Martin, the child's mother, had always liked to have a drink. Since the child's birth she had continued her daily trips to the pub wrapping the child up and leaving her on a sofa. With no fire to warm the room and nothing to eat the child then cried and screamed until she returned. Little wonder that the neighbouring houses were all too well aware of the child's presence and had begun to take serious note of just how badly she was being treated, though husband James, like his wife, seemed not to have noticed. From 6 pm every night of the week they stayed away until well after 11 pm and when they returned all the neighbours heard was a drunken mother threatening her daughter with violence because she cried so much.

Police Inspector Robert Tinkler, alerted by women from the surrounding houses, called at the court off Eagle Street, Derby on 14 October to see the little girl for himself:

> I looked through the window and there was no fire. Mrs Martin was at her mother's house. I went round there and saw her. I told her I had come to see her child. She took me into the front room. The baby was asleep on a sofa and the face was filthy dirty. The hair was clotted together and the nightgown was very nearly black. The under linen adhered to the flesh with filth. The child was in a much emaciated condition.

He told the mother that what he saw was unacceptable, that the little girl was in so desperate a condition. Sarah said that she had not been able to breast feed and had resorted to feeding the baby a concoction of boiled water, milk, bread and a little sugar. The policeman was disbelieving and told her so, insisting the child be taken to a doctor.

The following day Sarah carried the baby to a local doctor, Mr Gentle. He appeared not to have made a great deal of fuss over the condition in which he found the little girl and sent the two back home with a bottle of cod liver oil. But he did insist that the child be taken back to see him. Sarah ignored the request. took money from the Guardians to pay his fee and then went out drinking. This resulted in police sending their own doctor around to the house on Saturday 26 October but by then it was far too late and Annie Martin died the next day.

In court the couple were charged with manslaughter after police had learned that they had insured their daughters life for fifteen shillings. The payment had been demanded within hours of the death but the

Irongate, Derby c1890. Author's collection

insurance company had refused to pay until it was clear that they were not culpable. According to James Martin's mother-in-law Mrs Dreher, the woman who employed him two days a week in her drapery shop, it ought to have been paid. The child, she claimed, had not been neglected and it had been unfair of police to claim that she had not been properly cared for. She agreed that at certain times the child's covers and clothing had been soiled but that was not the normal state in which she had been kept.

Neighbours strongly disagreed. Bridget Chapman who lived next door to the Martin's told the court that the little girl had not only been neglected, starved and had generally existed throughout its short life in a wretched condition, but had also been constantly carried about the house and yard by 'a leg and a wing'. In other words by its mother grasping hold of an arm or a leg to carry her rather than in her arms. Others told of how in order to stop the girl crying out she would often resort to stuffing a rag in her mouth or resort to feeding her laudanum.

The Martin's of course denied all of this. Insisting that up until the last they had tried their best for their daughter. Spending time with her during the last night of her life in an attempt to nurse her to recovery. But those who knew differently were quick to stand up and say so. Evidence was brought in, which showed that far from nursing their sickly daughter, they had been in the pub at the end of Eagle Street until around midnight, Mrs Dreher included.

They were found guilty of manslaughter after the court accepted that they had allowed Annie to starve to death but that there had been no pre-meditation proven.

Chapter 13

The Cost of Life Insurance – The Murder of Kate Horton

1889

...he took the small bottle that had been so carefully hidden...

When George Horton and his wife moved into their little house on Swanwick Lane, midway between the small town of Alfreton and the village of Swanwick, it was meant to have been a move away from the cramped conditions they had been enduring for some years. Employed at Alfreton's new colliery, he had a regular income with which to fund his growing family and the move seemed sensible. At the time no doubt it had been and had the family not grown larger then both would have benefited from the extra two bedrooms they had gained. As it was the family continued to expand and by the summer of 1888, apart from themselves, there were another seven mouths to feed. Life had begun to take on a level of difficulty neither had ever envisaged. That difficulty became ever greater when in October of that same year his wife died.

Two of his daughters, Rosie and Annie, both having passed their eighteenth birthdays, moved out within months of her death to help lift some of the pressure from his shoulders. Financially it helped, particularly when he was able to rent out their room to Anne Bowskell and her husband Henry, long time friends of the family, but mentally it had almost no effect. By the spring of 1889, despite the small increase in his earning from these two lodgers, he was still looking for ways of easing his financial burden even further and after a fruitless search for additional work he believed he had found it. After meeting with John Wilde, the Refuge Insurance Agent for Derby and its surrounding area, he took out a policy insuring the life of his youngest daughter, eight-year-old Katie, for £7. He then began to plan her death.

In early May of that same year, some two months after that meeting, he bought a quantity of strychnine concealed inside a small blue bottle. He managed to keep it hidden away for some two weeks. Then,

The Old Toll Bar House, Swanwick Lane c1890. www.picturethepast.org.uk

on Sunday 19 May after all the family had spent the morning at the local chapel, he somehow was able to feed the little girl a small amount, possibly disguised in a cup of tea. By 7 pm that night she was complaining of severe stomach pains and was sent to bed. George Horton had presumed that she would die during the course of the night. He was very wrong. Katie survived and when he arose just after dawn to go off to work she called out to him to bring her some water.

Living as they were, three children in one bedroom, two others sharing his own and lodgers in the third, it was impossible for him to have avoided the fact that he had heard her calling. The Bowskells in fact had begun knocking on the wall the minute they heard Katie shout. Others in the house were already rising and in order to get to her he had to pass the whole of his family. Whether in panic or not he shouted back to her, complaining that he was late for work and telling her to get out of bed and fetch her own water. He then went downstairs. The water used by the family was drawn from a well in the garden and kept in pitchers in the pantry. That morning one full pitcher remained on the shelf. At some point, despite insisting she fetch her own water, he took a cup from the kitchen cupboard, filled it and carried it back upstairs. No doubt the realisation that he had not succeeded in killing his daughter with his first attempt had driven him to complete the task he had set himself. When he entered her room he took the small blue bottle that had been so carefully hidden and poured out its full content. There was to be no mistake this time. The unsuspecting Katie drank her fill and he returned the cup to the kitchen leaving it empty on the table before closing the back door behind him as he left, ostensibly for work.

Unfortunately for Katie her death was not instantaneous. What he had never realised was that strychnine acts rapidly on the central nervous system, causing violent convulsions that result in death from sheer exhaustion. Ingestion of the substance causes its victim to jackknife back and forth in agony, followed by furious and savage convulsions. On the previous night he had used so small a quantity that, of course, none of these reactions took place. But on the morning of 20 May he had emptied the bottle and as he left the house Katie struggled into the bedroom he had just vacated and where her elder

The Swanwick to Alfreton road today. The author

sister Sarah Jane lay. As she fell on to the bed she immediately stiffened and began to convulse. She was dead within minutes.

Henry Bowskell went off in search of George intending to bring him home from work. But George had never arrived at Alfreton Colliery that morning. Unable to concentrate long enough to carry out any kind of work he had decided that his time would be best served if he spent it alone. Taking a footpath through what was known locally as the plantation he walked aimlessly for about an hour. Then, judging that enough time had lapsed for his daughter to have died, he returned home. He and Henry arrived outside the house at the same time and the lodger told him before they both went in that the girl had died. Expressing mock grief and anger at not being there for her, claiming that had he known how ill she was he would never have left the house, George was extremely convincing. Unfortunately for him enough evidence existed to prove beyond doubt that death had not been by natural causes.

Police had the body removed and a post-mortem carried out by Dr Joseph Bingham was damning in the extreme. In the little girl's intestine he had found five worms some eight inches long, which could certainly have caused the stomach pains of the previous day but alongside this infestation was clear evidence of strychnine. Eight-

The Old Swanwick Colliery Road today. The author

tenths of a grain [51.8 milligrams] was found in her digestive system, half a grain would have been fatal. It provided irrefutable evidence that she had been poisoned.

George Horton was arrested and taken to Derby police station. He denied any knowledge of poison or of how his daughter had come to die. Strychnine, he insisted, had not been in the house or at least not with his knowledge or consent. He told the investigating officers that his daughter had wanted a drink of water that morning. He went on to describe how he had told her to fetch her own water and where the pitcher had been kept, adding that she must have found the poison herself and taken it in error. The house had its fair share of mice. He added that possibly there had been some sort of substance in the house that he had forgotten about that had been used to try and eradicate the infestation. Though he could offer no explanation as to where this substance, were it true, had been purchased, he maintained it was the only possible explanation.

What he did not know at that point though, was that police already had an explanation and it was one that was going to put a noose around his neck. Katie had not died instantly. After clambering onto her sister's bed she had managed to talk. According to Sarah Jane, the sister on whose bed she had died, Katie had told her that her father had indeed returned to the bedroom that morning clutching a cup of water. In a show of apparent concern for the eight-year-old he had then emptied into it the contents from a blue bottle with a white top. Katie had obviously been intended to believe that it was a medicine of some sort, which she did, drinking down the cups entire contents whilst her father watched on. There was no reason for her to question her own father's motives, but police believed it was at this point the strychnine had been administered.

Continuing to plead his innocence George Horton stood in the dock of Derby courthouse on 28 July before Mr Justice Hawkins, some eight weeks after the killing, and in a clear voice pleaded not guilty. On the face of it, all the known facts were against him. But he knew that none of it was any more than circumstantial. No one had actually seen him give his daughter poison, no one had ever seen poison in the house and no chemist had been found that could confirm its purchase and at the same time identify the purchaser. He believed strongly that the jury would agree with his plea if Katie's dying conversation with her sister could be discredited.

Defence barrister Mr Appleton informed the court, after listening to testimony from the witnesses to the death and its immediate aftermath, that nothing had actually been proven:

St Andrews Church, Swanwick. The author

> *...If the case for the prosecution was true, this was one of the meanest and most cowardly crimes that could possibly be imagined, because it was alleged that the father foully and cruelly put to death his own child – and for what? From no motive of anger certainly. It was said the crime was committed for a miserable sum of £7, the amount of insurance money due at the girl's death. The jury were being asked to consider a circumstance contrary to nature to commence with, and then there was no proof to show that the prisoner administered the fatal draught. In the cups there was no trace of anything of a bluish colour, and no poisons of any kind were found in the house. I do not deny that but a dose of strychnine had been passed into the girls system, but to ensure a conviction the prosecution had affirmatively to prove that it was the prisoner who gave it to her. I contend that the prosecution have failed in this, the most material part of the case.*

It was certainly a valid point well made. Only Katie's supposed conversation prior to her death added credence to the possibility that her father had been her killer. Absolutely no evidence had been found or produced that could link George Horton to the strychnine and no one else in the house, despite the cramped conditions, had seen him return to her bedroom that morning. There was therefore, perhaps in his mind at any rate, every reason to be confident that he would walk from the court a free man. But it was ill placed confidence. Too much damage had been created by the supposition presented by the prosecution counsel that if it had not been the father then who else could it have been? There could have been no one else. That single factor alone proved enough for the jury. They pronounced their guilty verdict after a short adjournment and George Horton was sentenced to death. Allowed the opportunity to speak to the court after sentence had been passed he said only that he was totally innocent.

A petition for reprieve was instantly launched on the grounds that no direct evidence linked him to the murder. Meanwhile, he was taken to the prison infirmary where he stayed under medical supervision complaining of ill health. The children with no adult to provide for their needs were taken into Belper Union Workhouse where they would spend the remainder of their childhood.

Alfreton Road today. The Horton's lived just beyond the traffic lights.
The author

When this petition for reprieve finally failed Horton wrote to his children imploring them to 'always tell the truth and trust in God', and requested that the elder daughters meet with him in Derby Gaol. The meeting took place on Tuesday, 20 August and in strained circumstances, the young women having been already notified that several days earlier their father had finally confessed to the murder of their sister.

On 12 or 13 August he told the vicar of Swanwick, Reverend Matthews, who had visited the condemned man on a daily basis, that he had lied in court and that he had been the man responsible for the murder of eight-year-old Katie. According to this statement the reason he gave for committing such an appalling killing was, 'penury distress and the fear of his home being broken up', adding that the strychnine had indeed been kept in a blue bottle and Katie had been truthful in her condemnation of him. The bottle he had cast away, apparently as he wandered aimlessly on the morning of her death, and the cup found on the kitchen table had been that used by him to commit the murder.

James Berry, executioner, arrived in Derby on the evening of 22 August to inspect the new scaffold, built under his direction. After consultation by letter with Derby's prison authorities he had insisted that they replace the metal beam from which the rope hung with one made from wood. This he told the authority, would allow more flexibility on the drop and help ensure the condemned man did not suffer the fate of strangulation. From a man who had executed over 200 prisoners it was advice well heeded, though obviously George Horton knew nothing of these plans.

On 23 August, twenty-five days after his conviction, he made the short walk from his cell to the scaffold, had arms and legs pinioned and was sent to his death within twenty seconds of meeting Berry for the first and only time in his life.

Chapter 14

Tragic Death at Callow – The Killing of Matilda Wardle
1892

'For Matilda it was a desperate and tragic two days...'

Matilda Wardle was only sixteen years of age when her mother sent her to the Ford family House at Callow to take up the role of domestic servant to the busy household. The family had known the Fords all of their life. Matilda's grandmother lived just down the road at Kirk Ireton and most of her other relatives either had work in Wirksworth, the small High Peak town no more than a mile or so up the road, or rented cottages there and worked for local farms. It seemed the perfect location for their daughter to begin her working life, near to those that knew her and employed by a family held in high regard by almost everyone that lived around the area.

Certainly from the outset all appeared well. Matilda quickly grew into the family's ways and seemed to have settled easily into the house's daily routines. She liked the close proximity to her own parents and enjoyed the small wage Mary Ford paid her. On her days off she often walked the short distance to her grandmother's house or into Wirksworth where friends would meet her. Most of these also worked in nearby houses as domestics and were therefore able to share in Matilda's workaday routines. They talked amongst themselves of the families round and about, their own troubles and squabbles and helped each other cope with the daily grind of domestic life. Matilda enjoyed the company; looked forward to their infrequent meetings and no doubt it helped her grow into the role her family had set her to. But things were about to change.

A year later and at some point in that late summer 1891 Matilda, whether by choice is not known, embarked upon a relationship with the Ford's son, Fred. There appears to have been no serious intent as far as he was concerned and certainly Matilda never discussed it. None in the circle of friends had any knowledge of it and she never discussed

The road leading into Callow as it looks today. The author

it with her own family. Fred did likewise. The liaison remained their secret but their relationship, perhaps as could have been expected, progressed beyond the purely platonic and by autumn had become sexual. Matilda, it is fair to say, had little if any sexual knowledge and when in February of the following year she fell ill she had no idea of the cause.

Concerned for her health and also apparently blissfully unaware of her son's involvement with the house domestic, Mary Ford took her servant to the surgery of Wirksworth's local surgeon, doctor Broster. It took him only a cursory examination to confirm that the young woman was pregnant. Matilda broke down and wept. Up to that point she had had no idea of her condition and, according to the doctor's later statement, refused at first to acknowledge the father. But Mary Ford, who, despite having lived in close proximity to Matilda and had not seen the signs, was insistent. Frightened of her employer, scared of the inevitable consequences, and no doubt at that moment feeling very alone, Matilda blurted out the whole sad and sorry tale. Fred Ford's culpability was out in the open.

Shocked at her own son's involvement with a servant, Mary Ford left the surgery desperate that her domestic servant's condition should never be brought into the public domain. Matilda, as far as she was concerned, was never to give birth to a bastard child that could lay the responsibility for its birth at her family door. Two days after the visit to Dr Broster, Mary had arranged for Matilda to be seen by a woman, loosely described as a midwife. The woman, Hannah Radford, lived over a herbalist's shop at 118 Friar Gate Derby. She and her husband John were known to have aided abortions on a number of women in return for one guinea.

Mary Ford and Matilda arrived at their shop on 18 February. For Matilda it was to be a journey into the unknown, and she had no idea why she had been taken to the premises or what was about to happen to her. She was told that Hannah Radford was a midwife who would simply care for her she was then left in an upstairs room and told, she would be collected later. But no one returned and after languishing in a bed for twenty-four hours, she was clumsily operated upon by a woman she had only met a day earlier, and a woman of whose medical expertise she had no knowledge of. Covered over in dirty linen in a bedroom scarcely furnished she was then left alone, after aborting her still born baby, until her employer returned to take her back to Callow.

For Matilda it was a desperate and tragic two days that would eventually claim her life. One week later and after suffering a deal of pain, Mary Ford was forced to send out for doctor Broster to attend the house. Unable to go himself, he in turn sent out his assistant, a Mr Reid, and he it was who attended her for the next three days. By that

The Derbyshire town of Wirksworth today. The author

time he realised that the young woman was dying, her internal wounds had turned septic and blood poisoning had set in. There was nothing he could do and he knew it. Matilda's father was sent for and told by the treating doctor to call in the police because he believed it to be a case of murder. He did as he was asked. Meanwhile doctor Broster arrived at the Ford house on 6 March 1892 and had Matilda removed to her own home where she died after giving a final and damning deposition to Superintendent William Lithe.

> *I, Matilda Wardle, of Callow, in the county of Derby, a domestic servant, being dangerously ill and in fear of death, make oath and say as follows: I am 18 years of age. I am a domestic servant with Mrs Ford of Callow, and have been with her two years or thereabouts. I found that I was ill about the 16 February last and on that day went to doctor Broster of Wirksworth accompanied by Mrs Ford, my mistress, to see what was the matter with me. The doctor then told me I was enceinte (pregnant). Fred Ford, my mistress's son, is the father of the child. Some few days after seeing the doctor I went to Derby by train from Wirksworth with my mistress, Mrs Ford. It was on a Thursday but I cannot remember the day of the month. Mrs Ford asked me if I would go to Derby. I did not know exactly why they wanted me to go, but I thought it was to give me some stuff .I went to a house in Derby...I saw a woman at the house. The next day the woman performed an operation...Mrs Ford came to see me at Derby about two days after the child was born...The house I went to had a shop under which had herbs in the window...*

John and Hannah Radford were arrested at Friar Gate the following day and their house searched. This in turn revealed a number of syringes and a bone knitting needle hidden beneath the mattress of an upstairs bed. According to arresting officer Detective Sergeant John Payne, the house was in an extremely poor state:

There were three bedrooms and a kind of garret. The place was very dirty and scantily furnished. Over the door was a sign on which was written, 'Professor Fearn, herbalist.' In the window there were bills, which previously belonged to Fearn, on which were written, 'Consultations free.'

The Radford's, it transpired, were not nor ever had been, herbalists. The sign had simply been left when they had taken over the shop from the good professor who had practised for a number of years prior to his death. It had suited them to leave it in place. Everyone knew the herbalist, which meant the shop was easily located by any that sought it. Hannah Radford had set herself up as a midwife and her clientele, who often came from outside of the town, had no difficulty in finding

The Red Lion Hotel *at Wirksworth where the inquest was held.* The author

her. Matilda had possibly been the first to die directly as a result of her ministrations.

The inquest opened at the *Red Lion Hotel*, Wirksworth on 14 March before the High Peak's coroner, Sidney Taylor. Lillies Via Gellia, of Ible, made the formal identification of the body. She had sat beside her aunt throughout the last night of her life and was simply best placed to have carried out the necessary legal requirement. Superintendent Lithe then read to the court Matilda's dying deposition and explained that the description of the shop in Derby, though brief, was enough to locate it and Hannah Radford, who shared the premises with her husband, as the woman that had carried out the abortion.

Dr Broster then detailed the extent of Matilda's injuries, which had been caused, in his opinion by either dirty instruments or fingers. Matilda Wardle, he told the court, had no chance of survival once her internal wounds had turned septic. Perhaps more damning, though less so for the Radford's, was what he insisted Mary Ford had told him about her domestic servant's injuries:

…The girl slipped upon some snow on the doorstep, and two days later whilst working at the slop stone something fell from her…

He told the coroner that he had not challenged that version of events but knew that it could not possibly have accounted for Matilda's injuries. Mary Ford had lied, not just about how the injuries had occurred but also about the way the baby had been aborted. And the local doctor knew it.

Probably for the sake of reputation Mary Ford did not want her neighbours to know of Matilda's pregnancy and had gone to great lengths to hide it from them. No doubt that was why she had lied to the doctor about just how her servant had suffered the injuries that had killed her. Police had noted throughout their investigation into the circumstances surrounding her death just how obstructive she had been. Even when they had discovered her part in the tragedy, she had refused to volunteer information. The court were told how Wirksworth's Police Constable Bradshaw had been obstructed in his enquiries and had only elicited information from her once she had realised that her attitude and actions could have been interpreted as being deliberate.

At the conclusion of the inquest, the coroner decided that, not only had her actions been deliberate, but that she had been directly involved in the death. He returned a verdict of murder against the Radfords and ordered that Mary Ford be arrested and charged with incitement to 'use the instrument that had caused Matilda Wardle's premature death'.

On 9 April, some four weeks later, she stood in the dock at Derby's courthouse having surrendered herself to police that morning. Her solicitor, a Mr Flint, applied for bail on the grounds that she had not committed the killing and was considered a woman of standing within the community. The magistrates agreed if she could offer up bail of 100 guineas (£105). Three farmers from Kirk Ireton offered their support and she was released.

No doubt this was a huge relief to both her and her family, though short lived. Six days later, alongside the Radfords, she appeared at Derbyshire's summer assize court on 15 April 1892 before a packed courtroom. Hannah Radford had been formally charged with murder, her husband as aiding and abetting and Mary was under a coroner's warrant for incitement. It was she that took the stand first. Prosecuting counsel wanted to know exactly what her involvement in the case had been. Just why had she taken Matilda to Derby and more specifically why to the Radfords? Mary broke down and told the court that she knew Hannah Radford to be a midwife. The judge demanded more.

Judge: *You were not ashamed to go there and arrange about all this? The shame should have come before now.*

Mary Ford: *No*

Judge: *What conversation did you have with the prisoners?*

Mary Ford: *I cannot remember what was said.*

Judge: *I will not allow the ends of justice to be frustrated, and you must remember what took place.*

Mary Ford: *I think he said his wife could not do it under 5 shillings.*

Judge: *If you really are ashamed of what you have done, you can atone for it to some extent by telling the truth now.*

Mary Ford: *I said that was too much.*

At that point cross examination began but Mary Ford had had enough and told the judge that in her opinion she had said enough and that she ought to be excused. The judge stopped the examination and in a severe rebuke told her in no uncertain terms that she had little choice in the matter:

> *…These people are on trial for their lives and you must recollect you have a great deal to do in putting them there.*

Reprimanded for her attitude and somewhat cowed into submission, she offered no further resistance and told the court what it wanted to know. As she left the stand, some half hour later, her ordeal was brought to an end. Prosecuting counsel told the judge that they no longer believed her culpable and that in their opinion the court should release her. There followed a legal argument and, after representation from her own counsel, the judge agreed. After a further admonishment she was released, but told to stay within the confines of the court.

Not so the Radfords, for them the day would be long in the extreme. Evidence was presented from a number of sources that proved beyond a shadow of doubt that Hannah Radford had received Matilda into her house, and also that her husband John, a blacksmith by trade, had been involved with other women who had been brought to the house and had secured money for his wife's services. What proved extremely difficult to demonstrate was that Matilda Wardle had been murdered.

In the defence's final summing up to the jury at the end of the day, their counsel, Mr Appleton, raised the lack of evidence that would categorically prove that murder had been committed. Hannah Radford, he insisted, had never denied her involvement in the case. Stating to police after her arrest that the girl had been brought to her in Derby by Mary Ford. Whether or not payment was made, he argued, was an irrelevance because it proved nothing. For Hannah Radford to be declared guilty of wilful murder the court had to show that she had committed an act that had eventually led to Matilda Wardle's death. This, he claimed, did not exist. Police evidence of what had been discovered in the house did not automatically mean that the items found had been used in any kind of operation on the dead girl. Her injuries, he insisted, could well have been inflicted at the Ford's house in Callow.

It was a powerful argument and one that was not lost on the court. No evidence had been produced that would directly link the couple with murder. Certainly Hannah had been practicing illegally as a midwife and her husband had either turned a blind eye or had shared in the profit. Both had met Matilda Wardle and some sort of operation had been carried out. But it was certainly reasonable to argue that no witness other than Matilda herself had been present when it took place and her dying deposition lacked key detail as to exactly what Hannah had performed on her person.

In his summing up the judge told the twelve male jurors that they must decide whether or not the death of Matilda Wardle had been caused with malice aforethought. The only circumstance upon which they could return a verdict of murder. He agreed it had been difficult to prove beyond doubt that the Radford's had been directly responsible for the death, but they had been involved:

They did not sit there to amend or criticise the law but to enforce it. The law was very plain upon the point and they may find verdicts of wilful murder or manslaughter, or they might discharge them altogether.

The jurors deliberated for thirty minutes before returning with the verdict of manslaughter. The judge congratulated them on reaching, what he considered to have been a fair and equitable decision and sentenced both Hannah and her husband to ten years penal servitude. Then turning once more to Mary Ford addressed her directly:

You are very lucky to be allowed to go. You have had as much to do with this as anybody. Go, go now.

Chapter 15

A not so Secret Affair – The Killing of William Preston

1921

Blood spurted out on to the road...

When John Lowe married his wife on 19 October, 1907 he intended it to be a marriage that lasted the whole of his life. He was in full-time employment with the Midland Railway in Derby and she seemed quite content in her role as housewife and eventually a mother. They rented a house in the city and like most newly married couples before and since saw no reason why they could not sustain their relationship no matter what the difficulties. Both had family living in streets nearby, friends to call on if required and a reasonably wide social circle. Over the next seven years those difficulties, when they arrived, were principally of a financial nature caused, in the main, by the birth of four children, not necessarily all planned but all wanted. So as 1914 arrived this small family unit was functioning well and not struggling too much for the key necessities of life. But with the year came the war and that changed things forever.

Twenty-six-years-old and keen to be involved, John Lowe joined the 2nd Battalion Notts and Derby regiment in August and for the next five years served on various fronts across Belgium. This left his wife and family, as it did many others, without the key wage earner at home and forced to make whatever decisions were necessary to sustain the families security alone. Left to her own devices his wife eventually took

Yates Street, Derby today. The author

the family to Yates Street in 1917, a move she saw as for the best. The terraced house was larger and more accommodating for her growing family and it was closer to the family help she often needed. It was to prove a disastrous decision.

Four doors away from number 42 lived the Kitchen family. At around the time of her move they had taken in their brother-in-law William Preston, 'Billy' to those that knew him, as a paying lodger. After serving in the 9th Battalion Sherwood Foresters, he had been invalided out of the army on full pension and sent back to Derby after being shot and seriously wounded in his left arm at Gallipoli. The nature of the wound was so serious that much of the muscle that gave the arm movement had been damaged beyond repair, leaving him with only his right arm and hand functioning effectively. This in turn restricted his employment prospects though, by the time of the Lowe's move, he had managed to secure a job at Rolls Royce. Described as a happy-go-lucky man he coped with his handicap extremely well and his army pension along with his new job provided him with a reasonable income, an income he also managed to supplement further by singing in various pubs around Derby or playing dominoes for money. But there was a darker side to his character.

Just what drew Lowe's wife to the man who had become her neighbour was never explained but by the end of 1917 they were heavily involved in an affair. He would spend large amounts of his time at the house and by early 1918 she found herself pregnant. It was not a condition she could easily hide and the whole street quickly discovered her secret and knew who the father of the child was likely to have been, but half way through the pregnancy she suffered a miscarriage. Fortuitously or otherwise it was too late to prevent her being forced to admit her adultery to her husband. No doubt devastated by the confession, he nevertheless agreed to overlook the indiscretion and forgave his wife. There were other things going on in his life at the time that perhaps demanded greater attention and no doubt he had no wish to return home to witness the break-up of his own family. Demobilised as the war ended in November 1918 he finally returned to Derby the following year.

As can be imagined, life at the Lowe household was far from happy at that time. The two had to repair their marriage, he needed to find a job and the war had to be put behind them both. But Billy Preston was an obdurate man and, despite the fact that John Lowe had returned to the marital home, he refused to give up his association with the man's wife. The affair began again and he became a frequent visitor to the Lowe household whenever opportunity allowed. Those opportunities increased after Lowe took a job with the Midland Railway once again, as an asphalter, which meant money was going back into the household, a fact not lost on Billy Preston. Despite not suffering any kind of serious financial hardship, he began to demand that Lowe's wife pay him on a regular almost weekly basis, something she inexplicably agreed to do though none of the money loaned was ever paid back.

For the next two years this strange love triangle continued. At some point John Lowe inevitably discovered his wife's renewed infidelity though not before it had once again become common knowledge amongst all that lived along the same street. There was the predictable confrontation between husband and wife, which did little to resolve their differences and an almost tacit agreement between the two that the affair would continue. Billy dropped into the background for a short while and then renewed the relationship on a more practical level, the two agreeing to meet on set days of the week. Secrecy no longer a prerequisite, no serious attempt was made to cover up these meetings and John Lowe, apparently accepting of the situation seemed to turn a blind eye. But despite this Billy began to view the husband of his lover as a threat he needed to eradicate. He built up a hatred of the man and took whatever opportunity he could to publicly berate and belittle him openly offering threats and talking to those that would listen about his wish to see the man dead.

In April 1921 Lowe was admitted to Derby's sanatorium. The nature of his illness is not known but Billy Preston cared little for the health of the man he hated so much and moved into the Lowe household within hours of his admittance. The couple co-habited in full view of the neighbourhood for the next three weeks, Preston only leaving on the morning John Lowe was due to return. It took no time at all for him to discover his wife's resumed betrayal of their marriage; probably he had suspected it would happen the moment he left the family home. Either way it had not been unexpected and neither had his usual forgiveness. The difference this time around was the fact that Billy Preston intended that the two men should resolve what he saw as their differences once and for all. He wanted John Lowe off the street, out of the house and away from his own wife.

The confrontation that everyone knew was coming finally arrived on 14 October 1921, though there had been other spats between the two, which Lowe had been careful to back away from without having to defend himself. When they met at 10.20 pm on the street in which they both lived there was to be no way out. Lowe and his wife had been drinking in the *Wilmot Arms* in celebration of his wife's birthday. Neither had drunk much alcohol, Lowe was not known as a drinker so, when they strolled back up the street and stopped to have a conversation with a near neighbour, they were both relatively sober. Preston, who that same week had been given notice to quit his lodgings because of his continued affair, was not. He had been drinking since early evening and when he walked back into his brother-in-law's house he knew that John Lowe was across the street. With only one thought in mind, confrontation, he hung his coat behind the door, exchanged a few brief words with his sister's husband and then strode back up the passage and on to the street.

Calling John Lowe names, he deliberately aimed a blow at his head, which missed but caught his wife in the mouth. Without any further thought Billy struck out a second time, this time catching him squarely on the chin and knocking him back into the house wall. At that point Lowe snapped. Just prior to the unprovoked attack he had been talking to the Priestley's, neighbours from two doors down. As they talked he had taken a pen knife from his pocket and as was his usual practice had begun to scrape tobacco out of his pipe bowl prior to refilling, so that when he struck back at Preston the knife was still in his hand. After a series of blows by both men they grappled and fell into the road. John Lowe's wife and Mrs Priestley tried to pull them apart and as they did so they realised that Preston had been stabbed. The knife, still embedded in his neck, protruded from just behind his left ear. Standing back, Lowe shouted at his wife to retrieve his pipe and then indicated the knife and, stooping down, she slowly withdrew it. Blood spurted out, on to the road, and as others ran into the street to help, Billy was carried back inside his sister's house where he died within half an hour.

The Guildhall, Derby today. The author

John Lowe was arrested that night and an inquest into the killing opened at the Derby Guildhall on Monday, 17 October but was adjourned after confirmation of identification had been received. The resumed hearing one-week later examined the case in greater detail and began by trying to unravel the complex relationships between Lowe, his wife and Billy Preston. A parade of witnesses found their way on to the stand and told what they knew, or had seen, or in some cases had heard, of the deadly triangular love affair all three seemed to have both endured and at times enjoyed. Eye witness accounts drew a verbal picture of the events of ten days earlier and police evidence confirmed the circumstances of the killing.

Dr S C Clarke who had been given the task of carrying out the post-mortem, told the court that Preston had died as a result of a haemorrhage caused by an incised wound 1.5 inches below the lobe of the right ear. The wound was some half an inch long and two or three inches deep. According to his testimony a great deal of force would have been needed to produce a wound of that type and in his opinion, it could not have been caused by accident. Only prompt medical attention would have saved the man's life and that, as the doctor pointed out, had not been available.

The coroner's jury returned the expected verdict of wilful murder against Lowe and the following morning he stood in the dock before the Borough Police Court. Lowe, brought to the courtroom from his Nottingham prison, stood throughout the proceedings between two warders. He appeared to those that saw him to be calm and spoke to friends with a degree of cordiality not often exhibited by a prisoner on a charge of murder. Whether he felt so confident inside is doubtful. Those that had testified at the inquest did so once more but there was a greater emphasis on this occasion in trying to unravel Preston's seemingly irrational behaviour. With that in mind, Lowe's sister-in-law had been brought to the court and testified that her sister, Mrs Lowe, had been afraid of Billy Preston. He had, she insisted, threatened her on numerous occasions and the relationship between the two was far from being what everyone had suspected. It may have been a sexual liaison, she insisted, but the sexual favours had not been freely given. Preston, she told the court, had used the threat of violence to ensure that he was never rejected and, despite this, he had also attempted to rape her on two separate occasions. How much credence the court gave to this testimony is not known but it certainly carried a degree of weight. Coupled with evidence of Preston's jealousy and open aggression it certainly caused the magistrates to rethink the charge against the accused. It was decided after a lengthy hearing that the murder charge ought to be lessened to one of manslaughter on the grounds that there had been no premeditation, so John Lowe was therefore, ordered to take his trial on that basis.

It opened in Derby on 9 November 1921 before Mr Justice Swift. Almost four weeks in prison had done little to dampen John Lowe's spirits but he knew that this was as far as he could go. If he lost here then he would spend years imprisoned for a killing he had begun to

The Cornmarket, Derby c1910. Author's collection

argue had not been his responsibility. The defence had built their case around the principle that it had not been John Lowe who had caused or forced the confrontation back in October. It had not been the man that stood in the dock who had embarked upon a series of adulterous relationships with another man's wife, and it had not been he that had intentionally plunged the knife into Preston's neck. Billy Preston's death, they argued, was to be regretted but he had sought conflict by instigating a showdown in the street. John Lowe had not been prepared for that showdown neither had he carried a weapon with which to defend himself. The very fact that the stabbing had taken place had been as a result of an accident, no more and no less.

When the prisoner's wife took the stand and told the court candidly of her relationship with the dead man she reiterated what her sister had said at the previous hearing. She was, she told the court, afraid of Billy Preston. Though they had undeniably been involved with each other for years she had endured threats to her physical well being and had been forced at times to pay the man money. Throughout it all, she told the court, Billy Preston had constantly levelled serious threats against her husband. Over the previous twelve months he had apparently tried on more than one occasion to force a fight he believed he could never lose.

When it came to it, the defence told the jury, John Lowe had defended himself as best he could. A man of smaller stature against a man who, despite having only one functional arm, was of greater strength.

The jury agreed and, in a rare event in a British courtroom in a trial of this nature, returned a verdict of not guilty. The crowds around the room and outside the building broke into spontaneous cheers.

Chapter 16

Allotment No. 48 – The Murder of Maud Atkins
1922

...it [the dog] *began to dig into a mound of loose soil.*

Percy Atkins met Maud Ekins in 1913 and after a short courtship married her on 10 January the following year. At first theirs was a good, solid marriage. Percy, having been a doting suitor had slipped easily into marriage and quickly became as dependable as he was hardworking. Just twenty-one-years-old when he walked up the aisle at the Friargate Chapel, he had all the good intentions required of a new husband and the two settled down to married life at 25 Francis Street, Derby. Between their marriage and 1921 they had two children, Leslie and Nellie, and to any that knew them they had grown into a long and successful marriage. Nothing could have been further from the truth.

Percy had begun to slowly drift away from Maud. Dissatisfied with the relationship, he had begun to spend time away from his home. In 1918 he had rented an allotment from the Highfield Allotment Society, which gave him an excuse to spend more and more time in his own company. It also allowed him to travel out of Derby, ostensibly to

Francis Street today. The author

buy plants and tools, which in turn afforded him the opportunity of building friendships away from the marriage. Centred on other gardeners, these friendships tended to be amongst men who shared a similar interest and were intended to aid him in his knowledge of all things horticultural. Unsuspecting of her husband's growing absences, Maud saw no reason to concern herself over these odd trips out and appeared content with the way her life was shaping up. Despite the growing distance between them, Percy had never exhibited any sort of violence toward her and the two of them rubbed along in a way that she thought suited both. Naivety was to be her undoing.

In September 1920, whilst visiting Bakewell, Percy met thirty-three -year-old Margaret Milton at a whist drive at the Co-operative Hall. Whether by chance or intent, he had partnered her throughout the night and she had enjoyed his company. Smitten, he returned two days later and partnered her once more but this time there was no letting her go when the evening ended. Insisting she allow him to escort her home he told her he was single, living in lodgings on the Nottingham road, Derby and working as a goods guard on the railway. She had no reason to believe he was lying and when he asked to see her a third time, showed no hesitation in agreeing. From that point on the meetings became more frequent and by spring of 1921 they were meeting almost every night of the week.

The unsuspecting Maud, despite the growing absence of her husband, refused to believe that anything untoward was happening to her marriage and it was not until early summer of that year that she

The Co-operative Hall, Bakewell. The author

was finally forced to confront her own suspicions. Percy must have realised that the constant trips to Bakewell were always going to arouse a level of suspicion he could never have explained away. He was right and, when that inevitable confrontation took place, the presence of Margaret Milton in his life came out. Maud's reaction was as would have been expected. Suspicion confirmed, she immediately left the house with their two children and fled to her parent's home in West Perrry, Huntingdon. For Percy the way had been cleared to spend ever more time in Bakewell and the arms of his willing lover.

Unaware that any of this had taken place, Margaret allowed herself to become ever more involved with the man she believed she would eventually marry. Percy, for his part, had managed to ingratiate himself into her family and the wider community. Accepted by her close neighbours and friends his visits were keenly awaited. No-one, he believed, knew anything of his double life and he went to great lengths to ensure it remained his secret. He had even managed to bring his two children into the relationship after forcing Maud to relinquish her hold on them and duping Margaret into believing that they were nephew and niece, that his own brother had abandoned them and that they were in need of a home. Young as they were, he knew that they were unlikely to contradict the concocted story and Margaret readily agreed to take them in. So, as autumn arrived with Maud safely hidden away in Huntingdonshire, and his children ensconced in their new home, he felt so secure that he asked Margaret to marry him.

Probably the notion of marriage had become unavoidable. Theirs had evolved into a long-term relationship and long-term relationships had an inevitability about them. Either they ended acrimoniously or else the couple bowed to social pressure and married. Percy chose marriage because he believed he had managed to build himself a new life and he saw no good reason why that life should be discovered by anyone outside Bakewell, particularly if he closed down his life in Derby. Neighbours on Francis Street had already been told that Maud had left home. He had also let it be known that he was to give up the house and move away and arrangements were in place to move out his furniture. He had been careful in just how he had managed the two ends of his life. All that remained for him to do, as he saw it, was to transfer himself from the one to the other as seamlessly as possible and all would be well. Maud, at that moment, seemed not to have entered either his thoughts or his future plans. Unfortunately for him though she was not about to disappear.

The banns were read at Bakewell church toward the end of October and, at around the same, time he began to move himself into

Bakewell parish church. The author

Margaret's house on Co-operative Street. Careful to continue his visits back to the house in Derby so as not to arouse suspicion he maintained the pretence that he had become a husband missing a wife, cultivating the notion amongst his Derby neighbours that he was both anxious and distressed about his situation. Even the allotment was carefully tended throughout this period, so intent was he to foster the belief that, despite his marital troubles, he would soldier on regardless. In Derby, at least he believed he had managed to hide his double life from curious eyes. He had not been so lucky in Bakewell.

A Mrs Keys who lived in the same row of houses as Margaret Milton had somehow discovered that Percy was married and had never divorced and four days before the couple were due to wed she had knocked on Margaret's door and told her, adding in the narrative that the two children were also his. Angry and feeling understandably betrayed Margaret in turn confronted Percy the same day. Caught unawares and obviously thinking on his feet he refuted the allegation, claiming that it was untrue that he was still a married man. Maud Atkins, he insisted, was dead. She had died of consumption at a house in Buckden in March of that year. Extremely ill when the two had split up over a year ago, he insisted her death had been inevitable. He had withheld the knowledge and the fact that the children were really his own, because he thought their marriage plans would have been dashed had he told the truth. Shocked by the admission, Margaret was nevertheless placated by his fawning performance of a man cast adrift by a dying wife. Convincing herself that the story had about it a ring of truth and not wanting to disbelieve the man she had fallen in love with, she acquiesced but as if to reinforce her acceptance she asked that he produce the death certificate. He agreed he would but added that, because his mother was holding it, he could do nothing

Co-operative Street today. The author

until after the wedding. Loath to embarrass herself by postponing the ceremony she let it pass and four days later, 14 November, they were married.

Maud meantime had written to Percy requesting they meet and sort out the house on Francis Street. He agreed and on 20 November, six days after his bigamous marriage, he met his first wife at their old home. The meeting was understandably acrimonious but the two nevertheless agreed that Percy could move whatever furniture there was to his new home in Bakewell. Maud, at that stage, believed he was simply moving away to escape the memories of their marriage, though there can be no doubt that she harboured suspicions about his motives. Whether as a result of these suspicions or not, Percy decided to tell her at that point he had become a bigamist. Incensed and feeling betrayed by his confession Maud immediately threatened him with the police. But Percy was nothing if not convincing when he needed to be. He persuaded her that his arrest would solve nothing and that it would create a far worse set of circumstances than those she was already enduring, particularly with the children. Somewhat influenced by his argument, she agreed to do nothing at that juncture and left him at the house.

On the following day at around 2 pm Percy had all the furniture loaded on a cart and taken to the house at Co-operative Street whilst

Maud watched from the street corner. The two then spent an hour wandering around Derby before he returned to Bakewell where he ate a late lunch with the, still unsuspecting Margaret. At four o'clock he was back in Derby and he and Maud met on the Nottingham road. After walking aimlessly for thirty minutes or so, he told her he needed to go back to his allotment, supposedly to collect some garden tools. She decided to return to Derby to eat and arranged that they meet up once more after six o'clock. They met for the last time near to the railway station, a difficult ill-tempered meeting that lasted for some two hours during which the understandably petulant Maud refused to be parted permanently from her children and demanded that either the two be returned to her or at the very least, if not both, then her young son. Percy angrily refused and in a fit of anger she threw her wedding ring at him in a gesture of defiance and ran off into the night. She was never to return home.

Percy meanwhile went back to his new life in Bakewell as if nothing had ever taken place. But things were about to take a turn for the worse. A relative of Maud's, a Mrs Cook, had grown ever more concerned over her disappearance. The two women had met a few days before her visit to Derby and because they had maintained a regular

Bakewell town today. The author

contact over the weeks leading up to the marriage break-down, she felt that Maud's sudden silence was unnatural. After making various enquiries as to Percy's whereabouts she finally tracked him down to the house in Bakewell and paid a visit. Unaware of Percy Atkins double life she asked the woman that answered her knock to bring Mrs Atkins to the door. A stunned Margaret announced herself as being Mrs Atkins. Seeing the two children playing on the kitchen floor Mrs Cook. pointed them out and told her she wanted to see their mother. What followed unravelled Percy Atkins life like a ball of wool.

Shocked into silence, Margaret listened as her visitor told her that Maud Atkins had not died a year earlier but had been alive and well three weeks ago, that she had been meeting Percy throughout October and November, that she also knew the two had met at the house in Francis Street when the furniture was removed. Desperate for answers Margaret had to wait until 7 pm that night when Percy arrived home from work. Trapped by the truth, he was forced to admit that he had lied and readily told what he dare of the last meeting on the 21 November. He claimed her disappearance to be as big a mystery to him as it had been to Mrs Cook, adding that he was not prepared to wait around, to be questioned by the police. Packing his bags, he left that same night and travelled to Manchester. They did not meet again for four days when Margaret travelled by train to meet with him and demand that he take his children with him. He agreed and after leaving her on the railway station took the two children to his mother's house. She in turn refused to care for both so the young boy he returned to Bakewell. Whilst there the suspicions raised by Mrs Cook and eventual fear of discovery by the police came to fruition when he found himself being questioned about Maud's disappearance. He lied of course, telling the investigating officers the same

Percy James Atkins attending his trial.
Derby Mercury

story he had at first told Margaret. He said Maud was in Nottingham Road Cemetery having died of consumption during November, just before his recent marriage. His new wife made no reference to the bigamy he had committed and so police accepted the story subject to corroboration by the cemetery officials. Not wanting to hang around after that he took the opportunity on Christmas Eve to make good his escape, all too well aware of what was about to happen next.

On New Year's Day 1922, Thomas Gore took his dog for a walk around the Highfield Road Allotments. When the dog reached allotment 48, the piece of land rented by Percy Atkins, it began to dig into a mound of loose soil. Intrigued by the shape this mound had caused in an otherwise relatively flat landscape, Thomas Gore went over to investigate. Two feet below the surface he discovered the fully clothed body of Maud Atkins.

The body lay on its left side. The hands and arms were drawn up in front of the face and the knees pulled in toward the body. There was a quantity of blood under the face and decomposition was advanced. She wore a blue grey coat, a bluish grey skirt, a green jumper, a black fur necklet, a pair of black lace up boots and a felt hat. Initial examination showed no outward signs of violence and there was no blood on any of the clothing. Atkins was arrested in New Malden on 3 January 1922 and brought back to Derby. He denied murder and insisted he had not seen his wife after 21 November when he had left her safe and unharmed.

The Canal Walk where Percy Atkins carried Maud's body. The author

Police never doubted his guilt and brought the case to trial six weeks later before a packed courtroom presided over by Mr Justice Horridge. Percy pleaded not guilty. From the outset it was to be a difficult case for him to win. He had invented so many stories over the preceding few months to account for the disappearance of his wife that credibility was always going to be an issue, and so it was. Sir Ryland Adkins who prosecuted for the crown laid out these various accounts of both her disappearance and apparent death before the jury, almost as a litany. But, with each pointed rhetorical question to the court, he succinctly highlighted the key facts as he saw them and ended his opening address with the one, single, known fact that Maud Atkins had met with her husband on the day of her death. It was all damning stuff.

A distressed Margaret Milton stood in the witness box some six yards away from her bigamist husband and, her voice full of anguish, related the events of the previous year. From her first meeting with Percy Atkins to the last in December of 1921, she carefully laid out the story of Maud as she had been led to believe from the various accounts he had offered her, and confirmed all his movements on the 21 November, the day police believed the murder had taken place. But under close questioning she had to agree that her version could have been incorrect on the grounds that she could not possibly be precise. Since she had found out that her marriage was illegal she had forced him to sleep on a sofa, therefore had he left the house during the night she would not have known. It blew a hole through the defence case. After other witnesses involved in the moving of his furniture to Bakewell had corroborated the police contention that he had met Maud on that day, work colleague, Henry Belderstone told the court that he had seen Percy in the company of a woman on Nottingham Road at around 10.30 pm. Belderstone was a reliable witness, he had known Atkins for four years and according to his testimony the two men actually spoke to each other as they passed in the street. If that woman was not Margaret Milton, argued police, then it must have been Maud. Either way it highlighted the lie in Percy Atkins statement that he had left her in Derby at 8.30 pm.

When Percy took the stand at four o'clock on the second day of the trial, having had time to reconsider his position, he gave a revised version of his original statement. Acknowledging for the first time that it had been he that had buried his wife in allotment 48, but insisting he had not murdered her. According to this new account he had left her after the argument over the children and despite searching the streets failed to find her again until he accidentally stumbled over her body beside the canal near to Chequers Lane Bridge. He told the court that after feeling for a pulse he realised she was dead. Panic seized him at that point. As a bigamist he knew that if she were found suspicion would automatically fall upon himself. He resolved to carry her body to the Highfield Road allotment, which he knew to be a lonely spot. Walking along the canal side he arrived at the Brewery allotments, turned into the meadow and so made his way to Highfield. En route he had to rest frequently but was never seen. He placed the body in a hole he had apparently dug out earlier to take an apple tree. After travelling back to Bakewell, he returned to the allotment at around 5.30 am the following morning and buried her.

The testimony was not believed. Dr Southern, who had carried out the post-mortem, told the jury that she had been suffocated after being struck on the head. The blow to the head would have rendered her unconscious but, according to the doctor, if she had been carried as Percy Atkins had stated, then she would have regained consciousness well before she reached the place at which her body was found, a measured distance of 1,359 yards. The injuries suggested that she had been killed after that original blow or had been placed in a grave whilst unconscious and died as a result of being buried alive.

The jury returned a verdict of guilty. An appeal was immediately launched but dismissed on 20 March 1922 and John Ellis executed Percy James Atkins on 7 April at Nottingham.

Chapter 17

A Forgetful Killer – The Murder of Ada Knighton

1927

…one of the strangest cases of murder to come before a judge.

William Knighton had lived all his twenty-two years at the family's home at 1 Bethel Street, Ilkeston, a house he shared with his parents, sister and a young nephew. Working as a miner at the nearby colliery he had a reasonable income, certainly enough for his needs, and no shortage of friends. Apart from the odd disagreement, the family all got on well. Since his elder sister had married and moved out they had also benefited from the extra space they had all gained. The house was small and to accommodate a family it had always been difficult so the more space they could create the more it was appreciated. Ada Knighton, the mother, had brought up her family well. The children had grown into young men and women with the advantage of a stable home life behind them, which she had always considered to be a priority. A good housekeeper, she had always ensured the house was clean, food was never in short supply and her skills as a cook were unchallenged.

Because of the numbers living in what was essentially a two-up two-down house they had evolved a sleeping arrangement that suited all. Father, because of his rather delicate health slept downstairs in a bed set up in the back room. William and his nephew slept upstairs and Ada and her daughter Doris slept together in a bed in the attic. None of them objected to the arrangements and had obviously grown used to it over the years. They had also grown used to the fact that as William grew older he had tended to spend more of his time in the local pub. By no stretch of the imagination was he a heavy drinker but a man who enjoyed the social life it offered and in particular, the company of friends, many of whom he had attended school with, that gathered in the bar each evening. So on Tuesday 8 February 1927 there was nothing unusual in the family having retired to their beds at a little after ten o'clock at night with William still out drinking. He had

The factory where William Knighton's sister worked. The author

his own key and was more than capable, though a little noisy, of letting himself in and making himself something to eat before he found his way to his own bedroom.

What made this night so very different was what took place at around 1 am. Doris had been the first to go to bed that night at just before 10 pm. Ada had gone out to see friends and she wanted the luxury of a bed all to herself for a while. The young nephew had been asleep for some time and the father of the house had been in bed for much of the evening. Ada returned at eleven o'clock and after making herself a cup of tea went straight up to the attic room carrying a candle to light her way. When William unlocked the back door of the house at sometime after 11.30 pm it was to a house in darkness. Whether he went to bed at that point is unclear but an hour and a half later Doris was disturbed from a deep sleep by her mother suddenly sitting up in bed and clutching at her back. Ada coughed a couple of times, then with a strange shudder lay back down. Still clinging to sleep despite the sudden movement beside her, Doris refused to open her eyes and as silence returned she began to drift back into a deep slumber. At that point she was suddenly pulled back to consciousness by the noise of someone opening the bedroom door. Opening her eyes she saw the dark silhouette of her brother William standing at the bottom of the bed. This was an uncommon occurrence. He had done it on several occasions in the past so she was not in the slightest alarmed at his sudden appearance. According to her later statement he appeared sober and simply asked her what was wrong with their mother. Doris put the time at around 1am. Still not prepared to leave the warmth of her bed, she told him to go back down stairs and instantly went back to sleep.

Five hours later at 6 am her father called upstairs for Ada to get up and start the breakfast. When there was no reply Doris, by now fully awake, got up and lit the candle. Walking around to her mother's side she saw blood pooling on the floor beneath the bed. But strangely she did not suddenly start shouting or crying out for help. Instead she calmly walked downstairs and told William, by this time seated at the breakfast table, to go up and see their mother. She told him that there was blood on the floor and she would not wake up. He did as asked but was quickly back downstairs to say that, '...there seems to be something the matter'. His father sent him back upstairs with brandy in a cup, which obviously had no effect and again he returned to say he could get no response. At that he was told to go up the street and

Ilkeston Town Hall. The author

fetch his married sister but he refused until he had had a cup of tea, which he duly drank. Only then did he fetch the sister (only ever referred to as Mrs Wake) but he did not return to the house with her. Leaving her at the top of the street he went straight to the police station met with Inspector Wheeldon and confessed that he had murdered his mother.

Describing the bizarre events of the morning and the discovery of the body of his mother still in bed, he told the policeman that he had no recollection of the killing. Finding a bloody cut throat razor in his pocket after his father had shouted up the stairs to rouse the house that morning was the only reason he had confessed. According to his later statement, after he had gone upstairs with the brandy he had seen for the first time the extent of her injuries. Slashed across the neck, which had left a gaping wound, she had bled profusely on to the bed and floor. At that point he claimed, he realised that if the blood covered razor were in his pocket then he must have been the killer. Startled by the sudden impact of his own guilt he had then dropped it under the bed and resolved that he must confess.

Subsequent examination confirmed what he had told the Inspector. Ada Knighton had been attacked as she slept and according to the post-mortem result would have died almost instantly. The razor he had left beneath the bed had been the murder weapon and she had died in the early hours of the morning. For the police it seemed an open and shut case. The investigation revealed only what William had told them and, had he not confessed, quite probably he would never have fallen under suspicion. No motive existed for the murder. No family disputes or argument were uncovered and as far as could be ascertained Ada had no enemies.

The trial opened in Derby on 26 February 1927 before Mr Justice Branson. Sir Henry Maddocks for the defence told the court that it was one of the strangest cases of murder to come before a judge:

> It is the duty of the jury to enquire whether the prisoner actually did it first of all; and secondly, if he did it, whether his mind was deranged. I am going to call him. He insists on being called. He insists on telling you that he believes he did do it. He remembers nothing during the night, but about 5.30 in the morning was aroused by his father calling his mother to get up. He got up and found a razor in his pocket with bloodstains on it. When he went upstairs and saw his mother's condition, he was in a fearful state because he believed he had done it. There was no quarrel. There was no motive at all. One wonders whether there was any intent and whether his mind was not deranged, not through drink, but through disease.

St Mary's parish church, Ilkeston. Author's collection

William Knighton then gave his evidence with quiet composure, reiterating in the main everything his defence barrister had just outlined. Three weeks after the murder, he still claimed to have no recollection of the event, only a self-belief that he had been the attacker.

There were no mitigating circumstances though it was shown in court that William did suffer from epilepsy. The defence team did bring medical evidence into the courtroom in an attempt to show that as an epileptic he could have committed murder without retaining the knowledge. But the science was imprecise and the jury ignored it. After an adjournment of one hour they returned a unanimous verdict of guilty and he was sentenced to death.

An appeal was instantly launched and heard on 21 March. Claiming that as a known epileptic the defence argued strongly that because no evidence existed that could directly link him to the crime a special judgement of 'guilty but insane' should be brought to bear. But after due deliberation the appeal was dismissed. A second appeal was then launched heralding new evidence. It came before the bench on 12 April. Doris Knighton, the sister that had slept with her mother that night, claimed her mother had begun coughing at 1 am and her brother William had not entered the bedroom until after that time. She further claimed that she had then checked and found Ada dead. The implication being that the only other person in the house capable of murder had been her own father. The court refused to accept the testimony and the appeal floundered once again.

William Knighton walked to the scaffold in Nottingham and was executed by Thomas Pierrepoint at 8 am on Wednesday 27 April. Whether or not he was guilty will forever remain a mystery.

Chapter 18

The Price of Debt – The Murder of Amy Collinson

1927

...an eagle-eyed constable found a piece of blood-covered pipe.

For thirty-two-year-old George Frederick Walter Haywood life had never proved either successful or lucrative. During the First World War he had served in the infantry but found himself transported to Egypt where he spent the whole of the war in an office and never saw a gun fired in anger. 1918 brought him back to Derbyshire and marriage to his childhood sweetheart, the two setting up home in Little Hayfield. After a spell of unemployment he became a commercial traveller for various companies, eventually joining Hazelhurst's, a Derbyshire soap manufacturer, in 1926. Life ought to have been on the up but George was not good when it came down to handling money.

By the end of the summer of 1927 he had fallen in debt to a number of people after a series of business ideas failed and was having a great deal of difficulty repaying what was owed. So he turned to theft. He embezzled small amounts of money from the sales of soap to customers. As most of his company transactions were carried out in cash the temptation to use some of the money these clients were

The Road into Little Hayfield Village. The author

New Mills where George Haywood collected his unemployment benefit. The author

paying him became just too great, though to him, the personal thefts he carried out were simple loans. Always intending to pay back what he took, he believed he would never be found out. He was very wrong. Never stealing on a grand scale, he nevertheless put himself into a position whereby he had to at all times account for all monies received on the due dates. It worked well for a time but eventually either over confidence or simple error caught him out. The company became aware that they were being short changed and on 11 October 1928 they sacked him.

With work scarce he had little option but to fall back on the state. Each week he travelled by bus to the unemployment office to draw the 25 shillings (£1.25p) he was entitled to and tried to find any work that he could do, no matter how temporary, to raise this amount to a level that would enable him to pay his creditors. By November he was desperate. At that point, he probably began to pay more than a passing interest in the businesses operating in the village, in particular the local pub. He was a regular at the *New Inn*, Little Hayfield, and his nights standing at the bar he began put to good use. The chit-chat, so common in all public houses he used to his best advantage. Slowly wheedling his way into the lives of the Collinson's who ran it until he was aware of just how much money the inn was handling and, more importantly, where it was being kept on a nightly basis.

Not that it ever took any large amount from its customers, numbers of which were always on the low side. Arthur Collinson, whose name was on the sign above the door as landlord, had been forced to take extra work in Glossop and travelled each day returning in the evening. This was an added bonus for George who by the second week of November had begun to formulate a plan to rob the inn. The knowledge that Amy would be alone in the bar each day only enhanced what he saw as success. But he knew that same success would be marred, if during the robbery anyone recognised him and the pub being in a small village where people's comings and goings were seen by too many prying eyes made that difficult to avoid. How to deal with Amy or avoid her in some way proved to be his greatest difficulty. A blocked sink, strangely enough, provided him with the solution.

On or around 9 November, the kitchen sink at home refused to empty. In an attempt to dislodge the build up of waste that was causing the blockage, his wife had taken a length of bamboo cane and forced it through the waste pipe. Unfortunately, despite the force she had used, her plumbing attempt failed. When George arrived back home it was to discover the sink still blocked and that the bamboo was firmly stuck down the pipe that was supposed to have carried the waste to the drain outside. His solution was simple; he sawed the offending piece of lead pipe off and threw it into the outside ash pit. But that is not where it stayed. Whether he had decided at that point or whether the notion came to him a day later, will never be known but certainly at some point he decided that the lead pipe was the solution to the problem of ensuring Amy Collinson could never identify him as the *New Inn* robber.

On the morning of 11 November, two days later, with that length of lead pipe in his pocket, he set out on his weekly trip to the

The Lantern Pike *formerly the* The New Inn *where Amy Collinson was murdered.*
The author

unemployment office at New Mills. He had already made the decision to carry out the robbery, steal the takings and solve his debt problem. The bus trip was intended to provide an alibi. Amy Collinson was not going to survive the day. She had only minutes to live from the moment Arthur Lomas and Mrs McBain, two people who knew him well, saw him enter the *New Inn* at five minutes past ten. She was probably cleaning out the kitchen grate when he struck her from behind with the length of lead pipe. As she hit the floor he then cut her throat with a knife and stabbed her through the neck with such force that the knife was left embedded in the floor. He then stole £40 in notes, calmly left the pub, locked the back door and walked up the street to the newsagent where he bought a newspaper, then crossed the road and caught his bus. The whole thing had taken no more than seven minutes and he had been clearly seen not only going into the *New Inn* but also leaving the newsagent, and boarding the bus. Quite possibly he had decided earlier that avoiding recognition was going to be impossible so he allowed as many people as possible to identify him being in the village at the time of the murder. What he had probably not intended though was that out of this eventual line up of eye-witnesses there would have been any that actually saw him enter the pub. It has to be doubtful that he ever realised that the two people who knew him better than the others, Mr Lomas and Mrs McBain, were on the street when he walked into Amy Collinson's kitchen. It would prove disastrous to him later.

When Arthur Collinson arrived home that night it was to find every door of the pub locked against him and the place in darkness. Realising immediately that all was not well he raised a neighbour, Amos Dawson, a man he knew to have a key and the two of them entered by the kitchen door. Amy of course was dead but nothing else in the place had been disturbed. Police were called in and within twenty-four hours they had managed to show that she had been alive up to 9.30 am that morning, when she took in milk from the local deliveryman but not after that time. There had been several callers to the pub after that time but none had gained admission. The pub had appeared deserted and empty. Police were also quick to discover the £40 loss from the hiding place Arthur and his wife had used each day. Intriguingly for police was the question of how this place had become known? With nothing else in the pub disturbed and no apparent search carried out they quickly hypothesised that the killer had been local. To know where the takings had been kept and to have only stolen the money, they argued, suggested a degree of knowledge a stranger would not have possessed.

So from the outset the *New Inn's* customers fell under suspicion and

Hayfield village today. The author

they set out to question each and every one of them, not a difficult task in such a small place and door-to-door enquiries quickly revealed the names of those that frequented the bar on most days of the week. Information gleaned from these enquiries also began to disclose people's movements during the morning of the murder, which inevitably led them to George Hayward's door. When first questioned he had been alone in his house and told police that he had called at the inn to buy cigarettes at around ten o'clock. When police returned the following day to verify certain facts, he was questioned alongside his wife. This time when he reiterated the same point she interjected to correct him, telling police he had told her that he had not been any where near the New Inn that morning. It was enough to rouse suspicion and the house was routinely searched. Very quickly the missing length of lead pipe was discovered as was £32 found hidden in the chimney breast. He was arrested and when an eagle-eyed constable found a second piece of blood-covered pipe inside the cistern of the *New Inn's* toilet, which matched that discovered earlier. He was charged with murder. Later investigations also showed that on the day of the murder he had also paid £2 to his wife and a further £4 to his creditors, money he was unable to account for.

At his trial in Derby on 20 February 1928 before Mr Justice Hawke, despite all the damning evidence to the contrary, he pleaded not guilty. Accepting that the pipe, which was the key piece of evidence, forensically matched his kitchen sink he continued to insist that he had discarded it after sawing it off and that it lay in the ash pit at the back of the house. Anyone, his defence team argued, could have taken it and used it to murder Amy Collinson. Wherever the money discovered had come from it could not be proven to have ever been in the possession of the Collinsons. Also, ran the defence argument; there had been insufficient time for Hayward to have carried out the murder. After taking all the witness statements that put him at or around the scene on the morning of the killing, they had calculated that only a seven-minute window existed during which he could have carried out a murder and a robbery. This they told the court was insufficient and therefore the crime could not have been done by Hayward.

Dr Homer Lynch did not subscribe to the view that it had taken so long a time to carry out the killing. He described to the court the level of injuries and the lack of defence wounds, which suggested Amy had been taken so much by surprise that she had no time to react. The killer moved at speed. So agreed the police, particularly when no search had been carried out and the money simply grabbed from its hiding place. The jury agreed and having obviously accepted that the pipe had come from the Hayward house and that money hidden away suggested theft, they returned a verdict of guilty.

George Hayward was executed on 10 April 1928 by Thomas Pierrepoint at Nottingham.

Chapter 19

A Spiteful Act of Revenge – The Murder of Mrs Kate Collier
1937

Taking deliberate aim he then shot her in the back.

When Horace William Brunt met Elsie Collier in 1935 it was, as far as he was concerned, a love match. Destiny he believed had brought the two together and Elsie seemed quite content when he began calling at her parent's farm at Wood End, Bradley, just outside Ashbourne. Two years later this potential son-in-law's regular visits ought to have generated a degree of familiarity with Elsie's parents reserved for those expected to join the family circle. But here Horace had only ever found the opposite. Elsie's mother, Kate Collier, had taken against him from their first ever meeting. This instant dislike, for the man her daughter clearly had a great deal of regard for began to cause a friction that became ever more evident as the years passed. Just why she felt so strongly opposed to the relationship she never explained but neither did she hide her hostility from those who knew her.

Horace Brunt, twenty-nine-years-old when the two of them first met, had lived a fairly chequered past when it came to work and it was presumed by many that this lack of any kind of security was the cause of Kate Collier's dislike. Having worked hard all her life on the farm, was (some said) why she had such a deep seated sense of animosity. His lack of endeavour and lack of qualifications or trade had often put him out of work. When he and Elsie began their courtship he had been

The road from Bradley toward Bradley End. The author

The Royal Oak Hotel *where Horace Brunt worked.* The author

working as a lorry driver with fairly regular hours and good pay but as with most things he got himself involved in the job came to an end. A short period of unemployment led to irregular work as a farm labourer and when that came to a halt in autumn of 1936 he was forced to spend a winter on unemployment benefit. This lengthy period out of the workplace obviously increased Kate's antagonism toward him and his welcome at the farm had,, by this time, been more than worn out.

On 14 April 1937, as spring spread itself across the Derbyshire countryside, Horace finally fell lucky. Offered a job as a yardman at the *Royal Oak Hotel* some three miles from the Collier farm he at last began to earn again. With 24 shillings (£1.20p) in his pocket every week, he was able to keep the wolf from his door and to take Elsie out on the odd trip. Life ought to have been on the up. But despite his brighter outlook on life it changed absolutely nothing in his relationship with Elsie's mother and that in turn caused friction between him and Elsie.

Nine days after starting his new job he resolved to rid himself of the irksome Kate Collier and the catalyst that caused this shift in attitude was a chicken pen. Since Hugo Collier had retired from full time farming, he and his wife Kate had begun a poultry farm. After a difficult start it had begun to show reasonable profit from the sale of birds for the table and eggs that were sold in Derby each week. When he arrived at the farmhouse on 23 April the two were busy trying to build a new pen for the extra birds they had bought in to increase their stock. The minute Kate saw him enter the farmyard she disdainfully turned her back on him and went into the house. Ignoring her ill manners Horace took his jacket off, threw it to the ground and offered to help with the building. Ungraciously, she thrust her head out of the back door and told him rather indignantly to leave the job alone, waving him away with a dismissive hand. She was going to regret her churlish attitude.

On the following day, at 11.30 am, Horace Brunt told Agnes Basset, landlady of the *Royal Oak*, that he had to have an early lunch in order to go off and meet his mother before she went into Ashbourne. It was a reasonable request and she had no objection. So he took his bicycle from its rest against the wall and she watched as he cycled away and expected that he would return within the hour. But Horace had absolutely no intention of travelling back home. This was a Saturday and Saturdays as he well knew meant that both Elsie and her father would be at Derby's Saturday market selling their eggs. The farm at Wood End would be quiet and Kate Collier would be alone, which was exactly what he wanted.

When he arrived at the house later that morning, the farm was quiet, as he had known it would be. Two years spent visiting at all hours and days of the week had developed in him a familiarity with the family routines that he was able to put to good use. It had also enabled him to develop a friendship with the two dogs that lay outside in the sun swept farmyard. This proved extremely useful that morning because he was able to take them into a back room of the house without them barking out any alarm. Once there, he locked them in and removed from the wall of the front room the little used shotgun kept by Hugo Collier. Carefully loading the gun with cartridges he had brought with him, he then very stealthily walked to the kitchen where he knew Kate would probably be standing at the sink. He was right and as he slowly pushed open the door and walked to the centre of the room she never heard him. Taking deliberate aim he then shot her in the back.

Kate Collier was killed instantly. She never saw who fired the gun. The shot hit her in the back of her neck causing her to recoil from the sink and land on her back in front of the open fire. Replacing the gun back onto its hooks on the wall in the front room he then stole all the

Bradley Church. The author

Upper Mayfield where Horace Brunt lived with his mother. The author

takings from the previous week's egg sales, some £9, kept in a tin in a place only his familiarity with the family would have allowed him to know. He then cycled back to the *Royal Oak* and returned to work as if nothing had happened and, just to reinforce this image of innocence, he went back to the farm later that evening, ostensibly to meet Elsie, and feign ignorance at the killing.

It had been the unfortunate Elsie that had first discovered her mother's body at around 3 pm. She it was that called out local police and by the time Horace arrived at six-thirty to offer phoney comfort, the officers were all around the farmhouse. The shotgun was the first item seized and easily and quickly identified as the murder weapon because it had been replaced on the wall the wrong way around and not cleaned after it had been fired. Police had also managed to show by nightfall that the cartridges used were not compliant with the gun, which led them to the conclusion that the killer had brought them with him. Questioned as a matter of routine, Horace denied any knowledge of the crime and insisted he had not been around the farmhouse that day. However, statements taken from locals during the preceding days threw doubt on that one single fact. Unbeknown to him two independent witnesses had seen him cycling toward Wood End at around lunchtime. They were to prove his downfall.

With the knowledge that Horace had lied about his movements police took him into custody and used the excuse to search his home at Rose Cottage, Upper Mayfield. Here they found identical cartridges to those used in the shooting. Coupling this discovery with the witness sightings led to his inevitable arrest on a charge of murder.

The trial opened in Derby on 2 July 1937 before Mr Justice Singleton. After five hours during which the court heard from various witnesses regarding both his movements and his strained relationship with the dead woman, Horace Brunt took the stand. A hush fell as he finally admitted to the jury that he had been responsible for Kate Collier's death, but in mitigation added that he had never fired the fatal shot. Over the past year, he claimed, he had fired the gun on several occasions and each time had replaced it on its wall hooks. The last occasion he could recall had been back in February of the same year but he was unable to say that he had not replaced the weapon unloaded. According to his concocted story he had gone to the Wood End farm on the 24 April to collect a pair of blue overalls. Kate was outside in the farmyard when he arrived. An argument of sorts ensued and he followed her into the house. As he walked into the kitchen she attacked him with a poker. A fight then followed and, once disarmed, she pulled the gun from the wall and struck out at him. He insisted that as he pulled the gun from her hands it fell to the floor and the shot was discharged that killed her. He had no explanation for why he had stolen the money but told the prosecution barrister that he had buried it a quarter of a mile away in woodland, still in its tin box. Bordering on the ludicrous he had no answer to the simple question, 'If the gun fired all by itself how did it shoot her in the back?'

But to add credence to the claim that he had lied continuously since his arrest, gunsmith Edgar Urton was brought to court from Chesterfield to refute the notion that the guns mechanism could have fired off itself. He did so extremely well, informing the court that in his expert opinion it would have been impossible for the gun to have been fired by accident. For Brunt the game was over. A jury returned the inevitable verdict of guilty and he was sentenced to death. An appeal was mounted within days and heard on 28 July but it failed. There was no new evidence in support of his claim and he was executed in Manchester exactly two weeks later.

Rose Cottage where police found the incriminating cartridges. The author

Chapter 20

A Very Jealous Father – The Murder of Winifred Stanley
1944

'I give her a good grave.'

William Meffen had always tried to do his best for his family and some would argue he had loved them all dearly. Others would say he loved one of them a little more than the rest, or at the very least tended to be a little too possessive at times. By February 1944 his family were no longer young, he himself was fifty-two-years-old and his three daughters in their late twenties or early thirties. His strongly held views on just how they should live their lives were out of step given the fact they were all adults and in some cases had married.

453 Nottingham Road, Chaddesden today. The author

Living at 453 Nottingham Road, Chaddesden, and working with two of these daughters, Lilly Calladine and stepdaughter Winifred Stanley at Derby Cables Ltd, meant that despite their dissent they could rarely stray from his ever-watchful eye. It was a situation he appeared to relish, particularly in the case of Winifred. For some reason it had been her rather than the others who had found herself more on the receiving end of Meffen's moralistic viewpoint and, as each year passed, he had grown ever more protective of her despite his wife's protestations, objecting almost as a point of principle to any man she associated with, always finding fault and refusing to accept any relationship she had tried to form.

So claustrophobic had Winifred begun to feel that she no longer allowed any of the men in her life, regardless of how insignificant or otherwise her friendship with them, to come into contact with him. So when she embarked upon a relationship with George Birks in the late summer of 1941, a man who also worked at the same factory, she did so secretly. For a while all went well and the two were able to meet unnoticed. But secrets of course have a way of being uncovered. Just how Meffen eventually discovered that his stepdaughter was becoming involved with Birks is not known; in all likelihood he was told by work colleagues or overhead a conversation, either way the objection was instant. He and Winifred argued bitterly over her new and blossoming relationship, with Meffen insisting she give him up. Winifred of course had earned the right, as she saw it, to decide exactly whom she went out with and refused pointedly to leave George Birks behind. So, unable to persuade the stepdaughter, he turned his attentions to the intended lover. He told Birks in no uncertain terms that he was to leave Winifred alone. He would countenance no association, no matter how innocent, between the two. But Birks, like Winifred, was not some young teenager all too ready to acquiesce to the demands and threats of an angry parent. He refused and told Meffen that he had no intention of deserting Winifred or of ending the relationship unless it was she that demanded it. The two men then continued to clash throughout the autumn with both refusing to give ground, culminating in a violent confrontation in November. For some reason Birks chose to call at the house on Nottingham Road to collect Winifred for a night out. It was probably inevitable, perhaps even sought, that he would be confronted by the indignant Meffen and he was physically ejected from the house.

Unperturbed, the two continued their liaison; albeit as far away from the irksome stepfather as they could, and on 22 February 1944 they decided to spend a night together. Too well aware of just what the repercussions would be if they were discovered, they chose the only place they could find, a holiday hut at Whatstandwell. It was to be the first time they had been able to spend time alone together. Yet here again, as had been the case so often before, the secrecy proved to be less than adequate. Though they managed their night away without discovery their attempt at concealment was exposed the following day. When Winifred had failed to arrive home that night an inconsolable Meffen had spent the night crying because of what he saw as

Winifred's betrayal. Forty-eight hours later and after a deal of pressure placed on those he believed knew the truth, he had managed to uncover much of the detail surrounding the clandestine arrangement. After seeking out Birks he demanded the man confirm what he already knew. Birks refused.

It mattered little; Meffen knew well enough the two had spent the night together. In a fateful decision on the night of 28 February, some six days after this humiliation as he saw it, he sat at the kitchen table and wrote out a note, which he addressed to the whole family:

Forgive me for what I have done, but I love Winifred, and she loved me until she got in with George Birks, and then the love between us was over.

To think a great man like him having for his wife a little one like her; it fills me up to think about it. I don't know when I shall do it, but it is bound to come, for I cannot stand it much longer.

He has made her as false as himself. Regards to Whatstandwell hut a week on Tuesday, it is true they were together, so I think I have done the best thing.

So mam, don't worry about me. Give her a good grave.

It was almost a death knell for Winifred. Having made the decision to murder her he then carefully folded the paper and replaced it in his pocket. To him her death was the only recourse left open to him. He could see no other way of re-imposing his authority over her life.

At 6.45 am on the following morning, 29 February, after an apparent night's sleep, Meffen walked downstairs to make tea then returned upstairs to the bathroom. Without announcing himself to Winifred who was inside, he pushed his way in, carefully locking the door behind him. Screaming out the moment she realised what was about to take place she made a grab at the door handle. But there was to be no way out for the stepdaughter that had defied her father. Larger, stronger and armed with a razor, he had no intention of allowing her to escape the tiny room. The fight was brief and, despite

Nottingham Road, Chaddesden today. Author's collection

his wife and daughter Elsie doing all they could to break through the door he cut her throat in two places. She was dead by the time the two women had managed to force their way in.

William Meffen made no apology for the murder neither did he make any attempt to harm his wife and daughter. Standing in the middle of the floor he allowed himself to be disarmed and said, 'No, I've done it and now I'll hang'. He then walked back to his bedroom, changed his clothes and left the house.

He did not walk far however, surrendering himself to the first policeman he met and requesting he be arrested saying:

> *I want you to lock me up. I have just cut my daughter's throat with a razor because she has been associating with a man.*

He was taken to Derby Police Station and there the letter he had written the night before was found still in his trouser pocket.

The trial opened in Derby on 19 June before a packed courtroom. William Frederick George Meffen stood in the dock and pleaded not guilty to the charge of murder. Since his arrest in February he had insisted that he had no recollection of having carried out the murder or of writing the note that was found in his pocket. Claiming that since his army service in India in 1909 where he had been infected with malaria, he had often suffered recurrences or bouts, as he called them, which caused him to lose consciousness. These bouts or attacks of malaria he insisted caused a loss of memory, which meant that he never had any recollection of just what had taken place whilst suffering the illness. Defence barristers Mr Norman Winning and Mr G A Myers-Ward built their case around the only available mitigating fact, that of insanity, and it was never going to be easy.

The prosecution alleged that because Meffen had written the note in which he pre-empted the murder then insanity could not be accepted as a reasonable defence. To declare that you are about to carry out a killing, they argued, meant that killing had to have been pre-meditated and if pre-meditated then insanity could not exist. Insane killers do not plan their murders. Ably led by Mr Walker Kelly Carter the prosecution further claimed that when William Meffen had forced his way into the bathroom on that February morning to kill his stepdaughter, it had been a murder fuelled by jealousy, caused by the stepfather's irrational fear that Winifred was about to be taken away from him by another man. It was a powerful argument and one he pursued through a number of witnesses including George Birks whose testimony regarding the numerous face-to-face confrontations Meffen had forced him to endure during his association with Winifred, only reinforced the argument.

Medical opinion was split however on whether or not jealousy had been a factor or simply that Meffen was mad. Dr G Waring Taylor, Medical Officer at Leicester Prison, testified that whilst it may have been that he had known what he was doing as he cut his stepdaughter's throat, it was also reasonable to assume that he suffered from a form of split mind associated with a hysteria. Mr Norman Winning tried to force a more rational explanation from the doctor.

Mr Norman Winning:	*Do you think he knew at the time what he was doing?*
Dr Waring Taylor:	*It is not possible for me to say.*
Mr Norman Winning:	*Do you think at the time he was cutting his stepdaughter's throat he knew it was a wrong and criminal thing to do?*
Dr Waring Taylor:	*It is possible, but emotionally he was so upset that his feelings overcame his reason.*

The first seeds of doubt had been sown. But the prosecution were not about to allow the notion of insanity to occupy the minds of the jurors. Dr John Humphrey, Medical Officer at Birmingham Prison, was brought to court to offer his diagnosis of Meffen's state of mind, which he did very succinctly, telling the court that in his opinion Meffen had complete recall of the murder and that he had exhibited no signs of memory lapse.

But it was extremely important to the defence team that the notion of insanity was not lost and that the jurors did consider it in their deliberations. So, as Mr Norman Winning stood before the jury at the closing of the trial he told them that there were only two possible verdicts in the case: *Guilty* and *Guilty but insane*. Powerfully, he argued that there was a high probability that Meffen was insane within the meaning of the law at the time he committed the act. Pointing to the dock he said:

> *He sits there with hardly an alteration in his expression, as though the result of this trial were of no consequence to him.*

Then with reference to the note written the night before the killing:

> *Is that the letter of a man who knew he was going to commit an atrocious crime, or the letter of a man who thought he was going to do the best thing?*

It was a well-constructed and compelling argument but not convincing enough to sway the final decision. William Meffen was found guilty after an adjournment of no more than thirty minutes and sentenced to death by Mr Justice Singleton.

He was executed at Leicester on the 8 August 1944.

Chapter 21

The Murder of a Corpse – The Killing of Ivy May Warner
1951

The bed around and beneath her body was completely saturated in blood...

When forty-one-year-old Ivy Warner walked away from her twenty-year marriage in October 1950, it could be argued that she exchanged her husband and the security of a stable relationship for the unpredictable, but perhaps more exciting potential, of a passionate love affair with a man she barely knew. Whether this is a fair assessment is not known, but certainly she had embarked upon a relationship with Derby machinist, John Eaton, by the time her marriage had ended. She had also taken rooms at a house in Hanley, Stoke-on-Trent. Hanley had been chosen because it was near to her work at Lancaster and Sandiland's Dresden works, a job she had held for fifteen years and one she was reluctant to give up. For Eaton, who lived in Derby, this meant the added strain of one of them having to travel whenever they wanted to meet, which in turn meant their meetings were less frequent than they had been. It also placed an added strain onto what was already a difficult sexual liaison. So, a regular visitor to Derby's *Carlton Hotel*, London Road, where he often went in the evenings for a drink, Eaton hatched the idea that every three months they would use the hotel as paying guests and register for

Midland Station, Derby circa 1920, where Ivy Warner would often meet John Eaton. Author's collection

one night as Mr and Mrs Warner. Ivy readily agreed and just to keep the romance alive, as it were, they also ensured that they always rented the same room.

Throughout 1951 this compromise worked well and during the intervening weeks they corresponded with each other on a fairly regular basis. If time allowed they also met outside this arrangement and certainly by the end of 1951 had begun to search for a house to buy. Ivy had set a limit of £850, which she insisted they could not exceed if they were to agree a mortgage and Eaton was actively searching out properties in Derby. All ought to have been well, but there was a dark cloud looming upon their horizon. When they met on 8 December 1951 in their favoured room, number 2, Ivy told Eaton that she was pregnant. It would be the last meeting the two ever had.

At 9 am the following day police sergeant Warren arrived at the hotel after a phone call from the proprietor, Mary Knowles, informing him that Ivy Warner was dead. According to his later testimony when he entered the bedroom she was lying in bed, the bedclothes pulled up to her neck, her face turned to one side and clear marks of violence about her throat. It was not until local doctor Walter Milburn arrived and removed the bedding, that the extent of Ivy Warner's injuries became glaringly apparent. The bed around and beneath her body was completely saturated in blood, according to the doctor several pints of it had soaked into the sheets and mattress and she had suffered three distinct injuries. A failed attempted abortion had severed a major artery, she had then been strangled and finally a pillow had been placed over her face to suffocate her. Eaton was arrested and taken to Derby police station.

Here he readily confessed to the killing and told police, 'I did it with my hands last night about midnight'. According to his statement the two had been drinking in the nearby *Green Dragon* and had argued after arriving back at the hotel room. What that argument had been about Eaton refused to elaborate on in any sort of detail except to say that there had been a deal of jealousy between the two. As to the murder itself he added, almost as a postscript, that whilst he accepted his own guilt he had no serious recollection of events, claiming that he had suffered some sort of mental blackout. After a ten-minute appearance in court the following morning he was remanded for seven days. One week later he was formally charged and ordered to take his trial in the New Year.

The trial opened on Wednesday, 20 February 1952 before Mr Justice Devlin with every space in the public gallery taken and queues outside Derby's courthouse of those unable to gain admittance. John Eaton, smartly dressed in a check sports jacket, cream shirt and maroon tie, took his place in the dock and pleaded 'not guilty' in a

DERBY EVENING TELEGRAPH, DECEMBER 10, 1951

Consulting
Opticians
ALBERT W. M.
WICHTMAN
(Opticians) LTD.
48, BABINGTON
LANE :: DERBY
Tel. Derby 45322
Hours: 10 a.m. to 5.30 p.m

DERBY EVENING TELEGRAPH
MIDDAY EDITION
INCORPORATING THE DERBY DAILY EXPRESS

No. 21,928   MONDAY, DECEMBER 10, 1951   TWOPENCE

Place your Christmas Order
Now for
OFFILERS ALES
and
NOURISHING
STOUT
We deliver in your district

COX & BOWRING (Derby) Ltd.
THE IRONGATES, DERBY.

DERBY MAN IS ACCUSED OF MURDER IN HOTEL

Remanded for week after ten-minute hearing

JOHN CYRIL EATON (37), machinist, of 117, Havelock-road, Derby, was accused at Derby to-day, of the murder of Ivy Warner, of 126, Eaton-street, Hanley, in Derby yesterday.

Eaton appeared in court wearing a grey open-necked shirt and a check sports coat.

Detective Inspector L. Shipton prosecuted, and Mr. A. E. H... ler appeared for Eaton.

The magistrates were: Coun-or H. J. T. Russell (chair-n), Alderman C. R. Bates, ., E. M. Lowe, and Mrs. M. ton.

Inspector Shipton said that at m. yesterday he went to the llton Hotel, London-road, 'by, to No. 2 bedroom, and on bed saw the body of a man.

... also in the room were Ser-nt Warren and Eaton,

I instructed Sergeant War- to take Eaton to the police ion," said the inspector.

The body was examined by Milburn who pronounced life inct.

The bo dhy was then iden-.. by the husband, William rner, of 8, Marina-drive, 'by, as that of his wife, Ivy y Warner."

MADE STATEMENT

Inspector Shipton said that .t he was present at a post-rtem examination conducted Professor J. M. Webster, of .. Home Office Laboratory, ... mingham. Later he saw ton at the Police Station, t after being charged Eaton de a statement.

At 4.10 yesterday afternoon, .pector Shipton said, he ..tioned and charged Eaton .h the offence. He replied, eged the inspector: "Couldn't i put 'telled.' I am guilty of ng it."

Asked in court if he had any ...ations to ask the inspector, aton shook his head.

Inspector Shipton then asked at Eaton be remanded in ...

'SHE WAS LIKED BY EVERYONE'

MRS. WARNER, who had rooms with Mr. and Mrs. H. E. Morris at 126, Eaton-street, Hanley, Stoke-on-Trent, was in charge of the paintresses at Lancaster and Sandland Ltd., Dresden Works, Hanley, where she had been employed for about 15 years.

QUIETEST NIGHT
Only five shots fired in Canal Zone

BRITISH authorities in the Suez Canal Zone to-day reported the quietest night since Egypt abrogated the Anglo-Egyptian Treaty.

Latest reports indicated that a total of only five shots had been fired. There were no casualties.

The Egyptian Cabinet will hold a special meeting in Cairo to-morrow to take a "decision" on Anglo-Egyptian relations. Last night the full Cabinet discussed the matter for four hours without coming to a decision.

The meeting was described as "momentous," but diplomatic circles in Cairo said that the Egyptian Government would not embark upon any rash action which might have far more repercussions than abrogation of the Anglo-Egyptian Treaty.

Under the protection of the British 16th Parachute ...

Mr. Edwin Sandland, director of the firm, said to-day "Mrs. Warner was liked by everyone. She came to us as a paintress about 15 years ag and just after the war she wa put in charge of the paintresses who number about 20. She wa a very satisfactory worker fro every point of view and we ar very sorry indeed to have los her. When she came to us he husband was working as .. potter in this district.

"A few years ago he went t work for the Royal Crow Derby Porcelain Co., Ltd., a Derby, and the home was move to Derby. Mrs. Warner like working for us so much that sh travelled from Derby each da until about 18 months ago whe she parted from her husban and she then took rooms Hanley."

POPULAR

Mrs. J. Jeffreys, one of th paintresses with whom Mr Warner worked, said: "Mr Warner was popular with a who knew her. She had a grea sense of humour and was ver fond of good music. She tol me that she was going to Derb for the week-end to see her J year-old d... ...r and ...

Newspaper headline of December 10 1951.
Author's collection

quiet voice. During the intervening weeks, as he languished in prison, he had reflected upon his original statement. Just before Christmas he told police that his earlier version of events had been untrue. In this second statement, the one his defence team brought to court, he claimed his assertion of having suffered a blackout had been false, made up on the spur of the moment. The truth, he now insisted, was that he had never murdered Ivy. It would have been impossible he now claimed, because Ivy was already dead when he placed his hands around her neck, the woman was a corpse when the murder was supposed to have taken place.

It was not surprising that the prosecution counsel, Mr R C Vaughan, Q C., did not accept this version of events. In his opening speech to the jury he told them this was such an incredible story that no jury could ever believe it. In order to be a corpse, he told the court, she had to have died and that death had been at the hands of John Cyril Eaton. The man in the dock had, he believed, both strangled and asphyxiated his lover after they had had sex in the bed in which her body had been discovered. The medical evidence, said Mr Vaughan, confirmed that

Ivy Warner's body showed signs that a great deal of pressure had been applied to her neck by Eaton using his thumb and fore-finger, which had left crescent shaped marks on the mid line of her throat. Similar marks had also been found on the back of her neck and on her shoulder. But, he claimed, none of these had actually been responsible for her death. A pillow, found beside the body showed clear indentation marks across its surface, which were consistent with having been placed upon the face of a breathing woman. Ivy Warner had been alive when that pillow had been placed over her face. The failed abortion, insisted the prosecuting counsel, had not resulted in her death and had taken place before either the act of strangulation or asphyxia. If John Eaton, he argued, had wanted to save the life of the woman he claimed to love then all he had to do was get her to the infirmary one hundred yards up the road from the hotel. The fact that he did no such thing was an indication of his intent. Powerful stuff and readily backed up by medical testimony.

But this was not going to be the simple case Mr Vaughan had intended it to be. The defence argument that Eaton had not deliberately murdered Ivy but had attempted to make it appear that a murder had taken place had some credence. In Eaton's first statement he had made no mention of the internal injuries Ivy had suffered, which they argued, showed that the statement was, as Eaton had claimed, a fabrication of the truth. The failed abortion had to have rendered her unconscious. The blood loss was such that she could not possibly have been aware of what was happening to her and, had Eaton simply left her on the bed, she would have died within twelve hours. The strangulation and eventual suffocation beneath her own pillow would therefore have been attempted upon a woman who showed every sign of having already died. The assertion that he had murdered a corpse was true, leastways to Eaton, and the reason behind that final outrage was simply that he wanted to be executed for murder. He could not live without the woman he loved and therefore endeavoured to create the illusion of murder in order to be killed himself. A counter argument that whilst appearing fanciful had some real merit. If medical evidence had supported the notion that Eaton had, in effect, created a sham murder, then his case would have been reasonably airtight. But, as Mr Vaughan had already pointed out to the jury, it was to do the opposite. From the witness box Dr Milburn, who had attended at the scene, destroyed any notion of pretence. Eaton, he insisted, had not only left clear marks of strangulation but had also used the pillow on her face not once, but several times, an indication that murder had been intended.

When Eaton took the stand on the second day of his trial he knew this one piece of evidence would destroy his case if the jury accepted it. He, therefore, had to convince them that he had never intended to take Ivy's life. Despite the medical evidence he needed to create enough doubt in their minds over the manner of her death by showing that he seriously believed her to have been dead when he had picked up that pillow.

Speaking in a low voice he told the court that the argument he had referred to in his first statement had never taken place. They had been on good terms when they had arrived back in the hotel room and the fact that Ivy had believed herself to be pregnant had come as no surprise. He claimed to have known for some time and had also known that Ivy did not want a child. The two had apparently discussed it at length on the night of her death and it had been her request that he help her terminate this pregnancy. That had led to her death. She, he insisted, had directed him on how to carry out an abortion and that it was during this failed attempt that she died. According to his testimony she did not shout out or make any noise but simply appeared to have fainted and he left her for a moment whilst he fetched water from the bathroom. Mr Walker Carter, QC asked him to tell the court exactly what happened next.

John Eaton: *She was still lying as I left her. I started to slap her face and shake her but she made no movement whatever. Then I paced around the room a little. I put my head on her chest to see if her heart was beating. I heard no beating. By then I was extremely upset and thought my world had collapsed. I put my hands round her throat hoping that I would be found guilty.*

Walker Carter: *Guilty of what?*

John Eaton: *Murder I suppose.*

Walker Carter: *What convinced you that she was dead? That there was no movement? At the time you put your hands round her throat did you believe her to be dead or alive?*

John Eaton: *Dead.*

Walker Carter: *Why put your hands round her throat believing her to be dead?*

John Eaton: *I wanted to be found guilty at the time of killing her by strangulation.*

Walker Carter: *What did you think would be the effect of putting your hands round her neck when she was already dead?*

John Eaton: *I hoped to make it appear that I killed her in that way.*

Walker Carter: *Why did you put the pillow over her face?*

John Eaton: *To cover her.*

Eaton went on to describe how, after the sham killing, he had been too afraid to tell anyone so had spent the whole night lying awake waiting for dawn. On the following morning he had decided that the police needed to be called and had plucked up the courage to inform the hotel and then wait to be arrested. This was his story and he continued to insist it was the truth. Whether or not the court believed him at that point is debatable but certainly Prosecution counsel did not. When Mr Vaughan, Q C stood on his feet before a hushed courtroom to begin a rigorous hour of cross examination, he knew he had to force Eaton to admit a falsehood or at the very least cast serious doubt upon the veracity of his revised statement. He began by questioning him about the failed abortion.

Mr Vaughan: *Are you saying you were trying to abort this woman?*

John Eaton: *Yes sir.*

Mr Vaughan: *And that in the course of it you thought she had died?*

John Eaton: *Yes.*

Mr Vaughan: *You thought you had killed her?*

John Eaton: *Yes.*

Mr Vaughan: *You thought it would be better that you should be thought to have killed her by strangling her? Did you realise all along that you had been directly responsible for her death?*

John Eaton: *Yes.*

Mr Vaughan: *So you desired this mockery of strangulation to enable you to be found guilty of murder?*

John Eaton: *Yes.*

Stoically, Eaton stuck to his story but when Mr Vaughan began to challenge him over his decision to change his original version of events he began to stumble in his evidence. The prosecution counsel accused him of deliberately falsifying his testimony in order to create confusion and doubt over his own guilt. Possibly he was correct but he had force Eaton to admit as much. When he began to question the reasoning behind such a radical defence Eaton began to flounder and stumble over his answers.

Mr Vaughan: *Were you looking for an excuse for having killed her by saying you had a black out?*

John Eaton: *I cannot answer.*

Mr Vaughan: *Was that in order to excuse yourself from having strangled her?*

John Eaton: *I could not tell you sir.*

Mr Vaughan: *Did you hope your statement about a black out might be some excuse for having strangled her?*

John Eaton: *I did not want an excuse.*

Mr Vaughan: *Why did you put it forward?*

John Eaton: *I might have read about it. It just passed through my head.*

And so it went on. The defence case was being slowly eroded and as the afternoon wore on Eaton found it more and more difficult to explain just why he had not sought medical attention for Ivy after the failed abortion. Nothing he offered up in his own defence explained away the one single fact, that after he had returned with a glass of water from the bathroom the bed was covered in blood. At that point, argued the prosecution, he must have realised that she was seriously injured and logic ought to have dictated that medical help was needed with some urgency. The question they raised was simply why were all the signs ignored? Eaton had no rational explanation, which left him wide open to the accusation that he had intended her death and that using the pillow several times to ensure asphyxia was a sure sign that he knew she was still alive when he first placed it over her mouth. Otherwise, ran the argument, why continue to press down over her face. On that point the case ended.

In his summing up Mr Justice Devlin told the jurors that the real question they had to determine on the charge of murder was whether or not they disbelieved Eaton's story in his second statement. He pointed out that there was some merit in the defence argument that murder had never been intended and that it was not impossible that Eaton did believe that Ivy Warner had already died by the time he placed his hands around her neck:

In the cold light of this courtroom that may seem almost incredible, but you must examine it by the darkened light of that bedroom, where, he says, his world had collapsed, and, in that state of mind, he decided what to do…But Eaton had then lain down on the bed and, if his story were true, spent 8½ hours lying on the bed, not asleep, in the room with the corpse beside him, and it was only when he was roused in the morning that he took the course of giving himself up to police. One view that could be considered was that he had spent those 8¹/₂ hours struggling to find some way out of the position which he had created and it was only when morning came and he had found no way out and he knew discovery was inevitable that he went downstairs and gave himself up.

He went on to question why Eaton had not sought help after he had realised that the abortion had been a complete disaster and then raised the question as to whether it were credible that, after looking for signs of life, he had then left her. But he was lukewarm regarding the pillow used to suffocate her because the imprints left behind by the shape of her face and mouth had obviously disappeared by the time it had been produced in court, a dilemma for the jury but one they chose to ignore. After an adjournment of two hours and fourteen minutes they returned a verdict of 'Guilty' with a strong recommendation for mercy. John Cyril Eaton was then sentenced to death. Luckily for him he was never to stand on the gallows. On 28 March, after a successful appeal, his sentenced was commuted to one of life imprisonment. It was a fortunate decision in light of the fact that Ivy Warner had never been pregnant in the first place.

INDEX